French Tales

For D.J.C.

French Tales

Stories translated by

Helen Constantine

OXFORD
UNIVERSITY PRESS

OXFORD

UNIVERSITY PRESS

Great Clarendon Street, Oxford OX2 6DP

Oxford University Press is a department of the University of Oxford.
It furthers the University's objective of excellence in research, scholarship,
and education by publishing worldwide in

Oxford New York

Auckland Cape Town Dar es Salaam Hong Kong Karachi
Kuala Lumpur Madrid Melbourne Mexico City Nairobi
New Delhi Shanghai Taipei Toronto

With offices in

Argentina Austria Brazil Chile Czech Republic France Greece
Guatemala Hungary Italy Japan Poland Portugal Singapore
South Korea Switzerland Thailand Turkey Ukraine Vietnam

Oxford is a registered trade mark of Oxford University Press
in the UK and in certain other countries

Published in the United States
by Oxford University Press Inc., New York

British Library Cataloguing in Publication Data

Data available

Library of Congress Cataloging in Publication Data

Data available

Typeset by SPI Publisher Services, Pondicherry, India
Printed in Great Britain
on acid-free paper by
Clays Ltd., St. Ives plc

ISBN 978–0–19–921748–9

1

Contents

Picture Credits

Introduction

First, the facts. These twenty-two stories are each set in in one of the twenty-two regions of France. I mean the modern regions, which derive from the ancient divisions of the country and often cover the same geographical area, not the *départements*, the smaller administrative areas, of which there are more than ninety, or the *communes*, which are smaller still. The division of France into regions was one of the main features of the French government's decentralization policy in 1982 when regional councils were set up and many functions formerly performed by central government having to do with the economy, social development, education, and culture were devolved to the regions. They have gradually become more important in the administrative life of France over the last twenty to thirty years.

Although Paris is in many ways still very much the centre of French life, a large amount of money is allocated to the development of all aspects of French culture in the provinces and in even small bookshops in provincial towns you will often find many layers of shelves devoted to regional stories and novels, sometimes in dialect or the local language, in Occitan, Basque, or Breton. Short-story festivals are held annually in many towns. The French are immensely proud of their *pays*, their country, in the local as well as the national sense, always eager to share what they call their *patrimoine*, a word which roughly translates as 'the cultural heritage we want to preserve and pass on to the next generation'. This idea, which arose in the eighteenth century, encompasses not only their art and architecture, their literature and folklore, but also their fine wines and enviable cuisine.

The richness and variety of the *patrimoine* of the twenty-two regions, celebrated in many French towns during the *journées du patrimoine* each year, is in part due to the geographical position of France in central Europe with its natural highways running between the Mediterranean and the Atlantic. Sharing a border with Spain, Italy, Germany, Luxembourg, Switzerland, and Belgium, France has absorbed and continues to absorb their cultures. Many diverse elements have gone into the making of the French nation, Celtic in the north-west, Iberian in the south-west, Germanic in Normandy and the north-east, and so on. Occupying armies, Roman, English, or German, as well as more recent immigrants from the former colonies, in particular North Africa, have, for good or ill, profoundly affected and altered the national culture.

The stories I have chosen for this anthology reflect this ethnic and ethnographical diversity. Thus, Christian Garcin's story set in Lille has Flemish associations and Mérimée's *Mateo Falcone*, about an honour killing in Corsica, is in many respects more characteristically Italian than French. The narrator's father and Jo's wife in Anne-Marie Garat's story from Aquitaine are immigrants from Portugal—many of whom arrived in the 1950s to try to make a living in France. Marcel Aymé's story, written in 1943, about Arbi, the Arab living on some stone steps at the bottom of a cul-de-sac in Paris, illustrates only too well the plight of many North Africans who came over to settle in the larger connurbations—Paris and Marseille especially—and Didier Daeninckx's story set in a twentieth-century Strasbourg, in the historically much-disputed territory of Alsace, makes a clever use of the German connections in the Second World War.

Some stories in this volume are by modern, perhaps unfamiliar, writers and some are well known to English-speaking readers. They are not arranged historically, and are in no way intended to be read as historical documents (my numbers simply run from 1, Brittany, at the top left corner of the hexagon, to 22, Corsica, at the bottom right). Nevertheless there is certainly incidental historical and social interest in the stories, and the collection as a whole mirrors some of the changes that have taken place in France over the last hundred years or so. Notably, at the beginning of the twentieth century, almost half the French population was in some way connected with the land or dependent upon it for their livelihood. At the beginning of the twenty-first century that figure had shrunk to just 4.3 per cent. Recent statistics show that more than half the world's population now lives in cities, and this shift seems to have had an even more dramatic effect on French than on British society. It goes without saying that many changes have taken place over the years in provincial as well as urban life as people have gradually moved into the towns and the countryside has become more and more depopulated.

These are the facts. But fiction is often much more enlightening about a country and its people than are statistics, and if we want to find out and understand what a nation is really like we must read its literature. Many great novelists have portrayed French society, and especially French provincial society: Balzac, of course, in his *Scènes de la Vie de Province*, George Sand writing of the Berry, Proust of Illiers-Combray, and many, many more. But the writers of *nouvelles*, or short stories, for various reasons which I shall try to show, although they do not attempt a panoramic view of society in the way that these novelists do, yet make their own particular and special contribution. They are *courts-métrages*, not the three-hour film; aspects and glimpses—not the whole.

The stories I have chosen are variously dramatic, tragic, comic, poetic, ghostly, anecdotal. The themes are timeless: the relation between humans and their environment; marriage and the dealings between the sexes; the nature of friendship; travel; the misery and the memory of war; buying and selling houses; honour killings; religion. All these matters still occupy and concern us today. I hope the stories convey the atmosphere, the feel, of a place, demonstrate the interaction of men and women with their surroundings, and show us how it is or how it was. Often there is a symbiotic relationship between humans and their environment, as in Hervieu's dramatic story of the shepherd and the bull. In the short story by Zola, the river Garonne, like the bull from Jouvet, is viewed as an attacking beast which must be fought. The writer's description of the flooding of the Garonne and its effect upon one family evokes in meticulous and horrific detail the natural catastrophe that occurred in the region of the Midi-Pyrénées in 1875. Zola based his story on newspaper accounts of this disaster which claimed around a thousand lives; and in that he rather resembles Dickens who, in his *Uncommercial Traveller* (1868), wrote accounts of real events in a variety of places in Britain. However, a story does not have to be as naturalistic as Zola's to reveal the horror or the pathos of an event or experience. Pierre Mac Orlan's poetic account of life in the Battle of the Somme belongs to a different writing tradition altogether: he gives us new insights into the somewhat surreal experience that it must frequently have been for those who fought in the First World War. For Mac Orlan the disfigured Picardy countryside resembles an 'exotic landscape in Tonkin'; a cannon may be disguised as a flowering apple tree and the 420 artillery piece, the largest of the weapons, looks like a diplodocus.

Many of these stories are 'travellers' tales' and were written because their authors, like Robert Louis Stevenson in the Cévennes, had good stories to tell. Travel, as is often said, broadens the mind; when you travel you meet people, you observe, compare, make connections, you learn—and if you are a writer, you may write a poem or play, a story or a novel about it. Maupassant, in his story set in the Auvergne, shows this process under way when he describes a woman sitting opposite him on a coach journey:

Yet you can't help observing her, you can't help your mind dwelling on her. Who is she? Where does she come from? Where is she going? In spite of yourself you sketch out a novella in your mind. She is pretty; she looks charming! Happy the man who . . . Would life be paradise with her by your side? Who knows? Perhaps she is the one to answer your needs, your dreams, your desires.

This woman is contrasted with the mother in the story's title, whose life-story the author subsequently learns, appropriately enough, in the ruins of the mysterious and dilapidated Château de Murol. Maupassant was a great traveller and walker—and storyteller—as is shown in both the stories I have chosen by him, set in the Auvergne and in Normandy.

Travel journals, or parts of them, sometimes turn into stories, and there is often a fine line between the two. This is the case with René Bazin's account, *The Saviours of the White Wine*, from the Loire region in the nineteenth century after the phylloxera disease had more or less wiped out the vines. This has a modern equivalent, for viticulture in France is currently facing, not a disease, but competition from the markets of the New World, a problem that equally threatens the livelihoods of farmers. Bazin is not as well known to English readers as Maupassant, but this tale taken from his wide-ranging *Récits de la Plaine et de la Montagne* will be of interest to those who want to know about the failures and successes of wine-growing in France over the last hundred and fifty years.

Travelling, though obviously not a new phenomenon, is very characteristic of our own age too; more people than ever are on the move. Travelling and learning about the towns and regions we visit adds to our appreciation of a place, and a good story can go far beyond the limits of a guidebook in enriching that experience. Stevenson's travels with Modestine in the Cévennes are memorable because of the adventures he recounts, the funny situations and characters he encounters, but mainly because of his skill in the retelling. Quite simply, he makes you want to go there.

I hope that francophiles will find plenty in these stories to make them want to go there or remind them of places they know. I hope the satirical stories of Maupassant, Daudet, or Daniel Boulanger, poking gentle fun at their own countrymen, will make them smile. And for those who love the countryside I hope they will find things to whet the appetite in these regional stories. Provence, for obvious reasons, has always held a particular attraction for us. It was especially difficult choosing texts for this region because they are so many and so diverse. I might have chosen something, for example, by Jean Giono, or Philippe Jaccottet, both of whom have intimate knowledge of its flora and fauna, and remarkable powers of evoking the landscape for their readers. But I finally settled on the two pieces by Daudet, partly for reasons of length and partly because in an amusing way they tell us a good deal about the folklore of Provence.

Daudet's *Lettres de mon Moulin,* purporting to have been written from a windmill near Arles in Fontvieille, achieved instant success when they began to be published in newspapers in 1866. Daudet, born in Nîmes, knew the landscape around the windmills in this area of Provence intimately. His description of his windmill as 'stuck on top of the hill like a butterfly', enjoyed by those of us who started to read French literature at school in the mid-twentieth century, is perhaps not so familiar to modern readers.

So too perhaps the story by Anne-Marie Garat, set in the less-famous region of the Landes in the south-west. The attraction of the little shack in the pinewoods is quite different from that of Daudet's windmill, but they have this in common—that the narrator is looking for a place to hide away from the world and have time for reflection, a subject which may also appeal to many people in our own overworked society. The landscape here is quite different from that of Daudet. There is a rather sinister quality in the long, interminable roads through the pine forests, but when her narrator describes the 'little beige and orange *girolles* standing up like bunches of flowers' in the walk through the wood that adjoins the house, or the stream with the fish at the bottom of the gully, we can understand why he is keen to buy. Sometimes there are unexpected glimpses of lesser-known landscapes. In *Julie,* by Jacques Chardonne, where there are striking descriptions of the Charentes, the post-war view of Royan, which like Saint-Malo was totally destroyed, is contrasted with the small town of Jarnac, 'the colour of pearl' and the landscape around with its 'slender jumble of branches in fine arabesques of Indian ink'. There are many other things to tempt the traveller: Maupassant's Lake of Pavin in the Auvergne is 'so round you would think it had been drawn with compasses'; the castle of Murol, ruined at that time, is 'a dead queen'. And in his story about Normandy he gives us a leisurely and vivid description of Rouen and of the river Seine as it snakes along at the bottom of the valley. Boulanger, in his story set in Lower Normandy, says of the pollarded oaks that they look like trees from the Bayeux tapestry and at once we can see those embroidered figures cutting down trees to make ships before the invasion of Britain.

It is often the telling detail or unexpected image rather than the raw fact that brings us up with a start and shows us what life is, or was, really like. Daudet's coach driver, for instance, addresses the narrator as 'Parisian' when he arrives at his windmill en route from Beaucaire, and thus underlines the distinction between him and the local passengers. I am thinking too, for instance, of Garcin's character Emmanuel, tangled up in the traffic of Lille, who 'has tried for three quarters of an hour to extricate himself from the usual maze of industrial zones which have spread like a cancer and circumscribe all towns nowadays, suffocating them beneath their advertising logos, as mistletoe suffocates old trees'. In the same story his character comments on: 'pedestrian shopping streets which all look exactly the same whether in Lille, Marseille, Bordeaux or Lyon, those paved streets with their interchangeable signs that have taken over town centres all over the country'. Though there may be small differences in the developments of urban areas, English and French alike will know exactly what he means.

Marcel Aymé, Christian Garcin, and Didier Daeninckx all set their stories in the urban environment, and, as we might expect, they are concerned with the homeless, the people who have ended up at the bottom of the pile in large cities. Karla, Emmanuel's girlfriend in *The Voiceless*, distinguishes between various kinds of homeless tramps, from the itinerant workers in the 1930s to the SDF's (Sans Domicile Fixe—of no fixed abode) characteristic of modern cities, who live in tenements, broken-down buildings or even tents and yet remain under constant harassment from the police. When looking for stories for this book I came across an anthology by well-known writers, including, amongst others, Nancy Huston, Jean-Marie Laclavetine, David Foenkinos, Jeanne Cressanges, with the title *Un toit* (A roof), with a preface written by l'Abbé Pierre, the priest and great campaigner for social justice who died in 2007. Despite the high standard of living, including health services, housing, education, transport systems, and other well-ordered social structures across the Channel, there is still a good deal of prejudice and racism and three million people in France still have no decent lodging. In his preface the Abbé speaks of a roof over one's head as a necessity to any life worth living. It is, he says, a sacred duty to provide this and knowing that writers also support his cause fills him with hope; but he also points out that the government unfortunately just changed the law according to which 20 per cent of all house-building by the commune must be social housing. 'It's a scandal,' he says. 'We must fight! If we can't accept that our children mix with those whose parents are disadvantaged, or those of a different race or culture, then we are teaching them to be arrogant, self-satisfied and insensitive to the fine values which are the very foundation of our Republic.'

A critical view of society is naturally implicit in many of the stories in *Un toit*. The one I have chosen, however, by Claude Michelet, is about a young bourgeois couple who are about to expand their family and move into a larger house, a subject which may resonate with many of the younger generation in Britain also trying to buy houses. In this very beautiful part of the French countryside there are many old houses in need of renovation, as well as many that have been restored, sometimes by incomers such as the British or the Dutch, but also by Parisians—who are still perceived as being wealthier than the local inhabitants and able to afford second homes.

Another powerful reason for writing about a particular place is the desire to remember, to make an act of piety towards the people who have gone before. Marcel Pagnol's Marseille trilogy (not represented here because they are novels, not stories) is dedicated to 'la mémoire des miens', and the home is often inextricably entwined with the place itself. Attachment to places is a strange thing. In times past we knew where we belonged, and like the Roubieu family in *The Flood*, we were much more rooted and knew where our allegiance lay. The country, the town, the village we call home or wherever we have that feeling of belonging, is a part of us, it has made us who we are. Some of the stories in this book eloquently express that feeling—Colette's *nouvelle* about her childhood in Saint-Sauveur in Burgundy, for example, with her loving evocations of her family and the garden which meant so much to her as a child; or Stéphane Émond's tributes to his ancestors who suffered in the war in Argonne in eastern France, in his book *Pastorales de Guerre*. Louis Pergaud and Jacques Chardonne both have that same attachment to their home regions. Claude Michelet almost always writes about his native Limousin, where he has lived and farmed, and Maupassant's satirical stories about Normandy and its inhabitants convey the particular intimacy, sometimes a love–hate relationship, this writer has with his home country. In others it may not be the native land that inspires a writer; the country of the heart may be elsewhere. Paul Hervieu was born and died in Paris, but nevertheless demonstrates a love and an astonishingly intimate knowledge of the mountains and the peasants who live there in *The Bull from Jouvet*, a tale which may remind readers of the powerful writing in *Pig Earth* by John Berger.

What struck me most forcibly when I read these stories was that they are as various as the regions of France themselves—varied in theme, perspective, mode, tone, and style; so translating them was a task that was both difficult and exciting in equal measure. Difficult because, as soon as I had finished translating one writer I had to begin empathizing with another, very different from the one before. Exciting because, as I translated, I found myself wanting to go there, to visit the place—was it the same or would it have changed out of all recognition? Perhaps these stories, even in translation, will have the same effect on readers as they had on me. Ever since my first visit to France I have suffered from chronic francophilia—that quickening of the pulse at seeing—or hearing—the names Montigny-sous-Chatillon, or Sillons-la-Cascade, or Les Eyzies-de-Tayac or . . . well, supply your own, you have only to look at the map . . . This anthology is for fellow-sufferers, who will know what I mean.

My thanks to my daughter Mary-Ann, who translated the two stories by Daniel Boulanger; to my son Simon for technical and historical advice; and especially to my husband, David, for his meticulous reading and thoughtful suggestions; to Olivia Mcannon for her inspiring photographs; to the French Institute, especially Hervé Ferrage, Sophie Moreau, and Paul Fournel, for their loyal help and encouragement; to my editors, Jacqueline Baker, Andrew MacNeillie, and Tom Perridge; my proofreader Debbie Sutcliffe, my copy editor Sylvie Jaffrey; and to Debbie Protheroe in the Art department of Oxford University Press.

You Should Have Changed at Dol

Annie Saumont

Tickets please, Ladies and Gentlemen, tickets pl...

The ticket-inspector's voice echoed rather oddly through the carriage. I raised my head and my book fell to the floor. I bent down to pick it up. It was a war story. About attacks and bombardments. A war that felt a long way off to me. I am nineteen. I shall be twenty at the end of the year 2000. Things that happened a long long time before I was born are what I call History.

The ticket-inspector stopped in front of me. I fumbled around in my handbag amongst my credit cards, mobile, packet of tranquillizers, and my small cosmetics purse. He glanced at my ticket. Then, rather sternly: You should have changed at Dol.

Oh, I said. I didn't realize, I said. What do I do now?

You are in a siding. There's nothing you can do. It's risky, dangerous. You seem honest to me so I won't ask you to pay extra.

He gave me back my ticket. He had gone to the far end of the carriage. Tickets please—for a moment I watched him. Then all noise subsided, I turned around, he disappeared. In my astonishment I let my book fall on the floor again. As I made to pick it up, a hand held it out to me, my neighbour's hand. A minute before, I had been positive I had no neighbour. There he was, smiling at me and yet I could scarcely see him, he seemed almost transparent. But I could make out his short-cropped hair, a tweed jacket. I smiled back at him. A rather wooden smile. When the ticket inspector had arrived I could have sworn the compartment was empty. Probably I hadn't noticed there were passengers behind me. But all of a sudden there wasn't a seat free. What had happened to the padded, imitation-leather seats? People were sitting on wooden benches in an old-fashioned carriage rattling along the rails. And they all seemed to be there and yet not there, they had the fragile appearance of people in a dream.

The conversation going back and forth between the *belote* players remains inaudible. One of them makes a silent objection. In silence the other lays his cards down. A woman with very frizzy hair is knitting with equally frizzy wool which she must have recovered by patiently applying herself to the unpicking of it. The four needles in the sock touch without the slightest clicking sound. In fact the woman is nothing but a shadowy form and the peasant woman with the basket of chestnuts simply a water-colour. A small child sucking her thumb is staring at me. She is pale, I have an urge to touch her and plant a kiss on her cheek. Something holds me back. I get the feeling any contact would be icy-cold. A man wearing a soft felt hat leafs through papers covered with writing. Girls with pallid faces confide their secrets to one other, bend their heads and whisper together, their hair demurely fastened back. One of them has drawn a line down her bare leg where the seam of a stocking should be. They are colourless, even the Soir de Paris on their lips has lost its shine.

Still farther off, a boy of 15 or 16 is on his own, biting his fingernails and glancing surreptitiously towards the end of the carriage where two officers in grey-green uniforms are sitting. They are smoking and seem not to be paying him any attention. They are chatting, or at least their mouths are forming words. Which I can't hear. The little girl is asleep, leaning against the woman knitting. A sudden movement from her mother as she drops her stitches wakes her up. She blinks and swings her feet, with wooden-soled sandals, back and forth. Her mother frowns but the teacher sitting opposite marking his papers makes a gesture of indulgence.

The well-shaven officer in the flat cap with the pompous little moustache takes a folded paper out of his briefcase. He opens it and passes it to his companion who asks a question, listens to the answer and nods. Both of them get up. The silent conversations are over. A brief glance around, then everybody looks at the floor, with the exception of the little girl who stares uncompromisingly at the officer as he makes his way to the end of the carriage. The boy hunches his shoulders, shoves his hands into the pockets of his jacket.

It seems as if the mist this autumnal day has seeped into the train. For me the rest is like a bad dream. I see one of the officers lean over the boy, who hesitates, then takes a dog-eared paper out of his pocket. The officer holds it out to the other one, who guffaws. I see the men seize hold of the boy. I see them take him to the guard's van. The teacher takes off his spectacles. No one moves a muscle. Only the mother stifles what must be a groan. I leap up, manage to catch up with the two men bearing their prey towards the carriage door. *In emergency pull the cord.* I pull. A screech of brakes. The train grinds to a halt.

I don't remember what happened afterwards. I was accused of interfering with the functioning of the train without good reason. *Any misuse will be punished.* I protested, I said I had been in a critical situation, it was a case of *force majeure.* It was no use me attempting to justify my actions, they retorted that being the only passenger I could not have felt threatened. I refused obstinately to pay a fine. I was not going to obey them. The Kommandantur. No, the SNCF.

After the court case I try to make sense of it. In Rennes, where I am studying, I consult the Archives. It takes several days of research before I finally light upon an article which contains some information. In 1944 there was an attack between Dol and Saint-Malo. They were intending to bomb the track during the night. A delay caused the tragedy. The little morning train was blown to bits, reduced to ashes in the fire. I was the victim of a hallucination, I must have read that article in my first year at uni in the course of some academic work on the destruction of the City of Saint-Malo—five hundred cubic metres of rubble in the war in 1940.

I went before the magistrate's court. *Knowingly and deliberately caused the train to stop. Refused to pay the fine.* How could I explain that on that October day a perfectly ordinary means of transport was transformed into a ghost train conveying ghostly passengers? They will think I'm mad. You can't say things like that. I did not ask for a lawyer. I say that I was feeling rather poorly that morning, I had gone to bed late the night before, I hadn't slept very well. I took pills—I show them the box—prescribed by a doctor, I read out what it says, *risk of drowsiness.* I say I was drowsy, that I had a nightmare. If in danger pull the cord. I thought I was in danger. The judge puts a question. What kind of danger? Insistent, can you be precise? I shout that they were certainly intending to throw him out of the carriage door. Who? The boy. What are you talking about, says the judge. I mumble, No it was in my dream. The judge stares at me, You must learn to be wary of dreams. In his eyes I read some kind of a warning. He puts my file in the pending tray. His hand shakes. His nails are bitten.

He sentences me to one month's community service. Extenuating circumstances give me the right to defer my punishment till the summer vacation, my studies will not be adversely affected.

My summons comes in July. You will report to the community restaurant in Saint-Malo. You will complete five hours waitressing and dishwashing every day. You must register every day.

When I went to the station to find out the train times the employee at the ticket office calmly declared, No no, you don't change at Dol. She was tinkling away at her piano. I said, Okay, thanks.

I went by bus.

I arrive at the address I was given. It's behind the ramparts, near the Law Courts, below the Enclos de la Résistance. A four-storey building with a lovely granite exterior, no sign outside. Nothing to indicate the existence of a sub-sidized restaurant providing the least well-off with cheap meals. I've read articles on soup-kitchens in the war. Do people still talk about 'soup kitchens?' All you hear about nowadays is souped-up restaurants.

A man working on the pavement has lifted the cover off a drain and is preparing to go down inside. I hurry over to ask him something. I ask. I insist, I invent. It's about a vac job. Really? says the man. Who sent you? They must have gone dotty. The community restaurant was destroyed at the end of the war. When the whole town was burned. They rebuilt it in granite, stone lasts, towns can be rebuilt, life goes on but people die, things change. The people who sent you here can't be right in the head. He says he doesn't know any details, wasn't there, wasn't born then. He was told the town was evacuated. The ones who insisted on staying all piled into shelters. They only came out for their eats. When the Yanks stepped up their attacks the soup-kitchen was hit by an incendiary.

The man checked the ladder, was swallowed up by the hole and the cover closed over him. I called the court in Rennes. The secretary hesitated, then said that the judge had just unexpectedly gone on leave. For personal reasons. I would receive another placement in due course.

The seagulls are making an enormous din.

It's summer, I go down to the shore, I take my book but don't read. I take my notes but don't study. I sit with my back to the jetty. I wait. I contemplate the sea and I swallow my little pink-and-white pills.

Made for Two

Daniel Boulanger

That day my wife and I were out for a walk in the countryside around Bayeux, where the pollarded oaks look like
trees from the famous tapestry. At about four in the afternoon we took a little leaf-strewn path down to the old
church of Thaon, which sits like a shrine lost in the woods,
and we lay down by one of the gravestones planted along
one side. Not a single walker, not one single bird, only a
silence like the sound of water and a sky as flat as a lily pad.

When we got back to the road where we had left our
car we came across a man who was perhaps in his sixties,
sitting on the bank, a long umbrella between his legs. He
peered at us from behind a red, hairy nose, heavy in his

Sunday clothes—a frock coat with its skirts lifted and a pair of solid-heeled boots rubbing against his pasty shins.

Astonished to see him all got up like that with a gold pin in his cravat, and in such an out-of-the-way place, my wife murmured:

'I wouldn't mind seeing the rest of the funeral.'

She was wrong, but not by much.

He gave us a good looking over, our man, his big eyes popping. Thin hair stuck with sweat flicked out over his temples, and he held his hat with its rolled-up edges and the long umbrella between his parted legs.

We got into the car.

'Can I help you at all?' I said. 'Are you going to the next village? Do get in!'

'I've got plenty of time,' he replied.

'Oh, excuse me.'

'Your wife?' He lifted the umbrella.

'My wife, yes.'

He had a Norman accent and a rounded, slightly acerbic voice. His eyes were focused on the tips of his big boots with their tiny concertina folds.

'Be happy!' he shouted across at us.

'We try.'

'Easier if you're two. I was two once. We had a little farm near Falaise, five cows and a daughter. The daughter is in England with a man in coal, he came over with the others in forty-four. Wife didn't like him much. The daughter went off with him a year later. He was a bomb disposal expert. The Germans had mined all around our place. There was a little path from the house to the wash-house. And there's my wife going down it one morning with the wheelbarrow. Done it maybe five hundred times since the war. And that day, Monsieur, a mine. All I found was the clothes, the clothes she was going to wash, the clothes she was wearing. Nothing left of her, almost nothing. So there I am alone. I sold the cows first. My daughter couldn't make it over for the service. And she never liked it round here. I'm getting old, I can't stay like this. So for the last two years I've been scouring the area for a companion. I went as far as the sea, all the way to Laigle, always on foot. I watch. The little roads. The big roads. When I see a woman by herself, about my age, I strike up a conversation. Once it nearly worked out. You wouldn't believe it, but it was just next door to me, the other side of Falaise! And I'd already done eight or nine hundred kilometres at least, and then it didn't work out after all. She said I would always be thinking of the other one, of my dead wife, and that she'd be the same except her husband didn't die from a mine, but at Sées, off some scaffolding. And there was another time I found one. She ran a little bar, but I could see she had plenty of admirers. So I push on, I've got time, I'll find one in the end.'

He stopped, his brow raised.

'How about a drink in the next place?' I asked.

'I have my companion,' he said, pulling a half-litre bottle of alcohol out of his pocket. 'You want to try it?'

'How far do you walk each day?'

'Depends. Sometimes twenty, sometimes thirty, sometimes less. It depends on what I find. I do the villages too, but there's not much to be had in villages. Towns are better, but you need time for those. I don't want to miss anything.'

'Well,' I said. 'Best of luck!'

'Oh, my legs are strong enough. If only they knew! *Foi de Guillaume.*' (He pronounced it *Guïliaume*).

'Like the Conqueror?'

'And from the very same town, Monsieur. They've made a statue for him, you should see it. One big block of stone right down to the horse's tail, it's a great work.'

We looked at the old man's costume. He really was the perfect country suitor, a man of sentiment, dressed up to the nines with that splendid gold pin and, ready to hand, his bottle, the glorious badge of his vice...

He put his hat back on; its band was almost purple with age.

'I'll find one,' he said. 'I was made to be two.'

When we left he stood up. On our way down the road, just before he disappeared behind the tall grasses and the hedges, we stopped and made him a grand gesture of farewell. Small and paunchy, he lifted his hat.

'Be happy,' my wife said quietly. I took her hand.

A Norman

Guy de Maupassant
for Paul Alexis

We had just left Rouen and were going at a cracking pace along the road to Jumièges. The coach passed swiftly across the grassy plain and then the horse slowed to a walk as he went up the hill at Canteleu.

It was one of the most wonderful panoramas in the world. Behind us, Rouen, the city of churches, with its Gothic towers, intricate as ivories; in front of us, Saint-Sever, the manufacturing suburb with its thousand smoking chimneys rising up against the vast sky, opposite the thousand holy belltowers of the ancient city.

Here was the spire of the cathedral, the greatest of all mankind's achievements; over there the 'Fire pump' of the

'Thunderer', its rival, almost as excessive, one metre higher than the pyramids of Egypt.

And the Seine, winding and flowing along down below us, dotted with little islands, bordered on the right by tree-covered white cliffs, and, to the left, by an immense grassy plain which ended in another forest in the far, far distance . . .

Here and there big ships were at anchor along the wide river-banks. Three great steamboats were setting off, one behind the other, towards Le Havre; and a string of vessels—a three-masted ship, two schooners, and a brig going back to Rouen—were being towed by a small tugboat belching clouds of black smoke.

My companion, a native of the region, was not looking at this surprising landscape at all; but he had a perpetual smile on his face, as if enjoying a private joke. Then, suddenly:

'I'm going to show you something', said he, 'that'll really make you laugh. Father Mathieu's chapel. You'll love it!'

I looked at him, amazed.

'I shall give you a flavour of Normandy', he went on, 'which will stay with you for ever. Father Mathieu is the finest Norman in the region and his chapel is one of the wonders of the world, no more, no less. But first, a few words of explanation.

'Father Mathieu, also known as "Father Boozer", is a former sergeant-major who has returned to his native land. He possesses in equal measure the old soldier's fondness for a joke and a wily Norman impishness—a perfectly admirable combination. Now home again, he has become the custodian, thanks to a fair amount of influence and some extremely smart moves on his part, of a chapel of miracles, a chapel which is under the protection of the Virgin and frequented in the main by pregnant girls. He has baptized his miraculous statue with the name "Our Lady of the Fat Belly" and he treats her with a certain joking familiarity not at all lacking in respect. He has even composed and had printed a special prayer for his HOLY VIRGIN. This prayer is a masterpiece of unintended irony and Norman wit, in which mockery rubs shoulders with a fear of the Saint, a superstitious fear of some hidden powers. He does not believe all that much in his patron, but he does believe in her a little, because he is prudent, and he handles her carefully, because it is in his interest to do so.

'Here is the beginning of this astonishing prayer:

"Our good lady Virgin Mary, natural patroness of unmarried mothers in this land and on all the earth, protect this your servant who has sinned in a moment of forgetfulness...." And this is how the supplication ends:

"Remember me especially when you are with your blessed husband and intercede for me with God the Father, that He may grant me a good husband like yours."

'Though this prayer is forbidden by the clergy of the region, it is sold by him on the quiet, and held to be efficacious for all the women who recite it with feeling.

'In other words, he speaks of the Virgin just as a manservant might speak of a prince, his redoubtable master, being as it were party to all his intimate secrets. He knows innumerable funny stories about her and recounts them *sotto voce* when he is with friends and after he has had one or two drinks.

'But you will see for yourself.

'Because the income from his patron, the Virgin, does not provide for him adequately, he has expanded his business with a little shop that sells saints. He has stocks of all, or nearly all, of them. Since he is short of space in the chapel he has set up a stall in the woodshed and goes and gets them from there as soon as one of the faithful asks. He has carved these little statues out of wood himself; they are unbelievably comic. One year when he was having his house daubed, he painted them all bright green. As you know, saints cure illnesses. Each has his or her own particular malady, and one must not mix them up or get it wrong. They are as jealous as actors of one another.

'The old biddies come and consult Mathieu, so as not to make a mistake.

"What saint is best for earache?"

"Saint Osymus is good, but there's also Saint Pamphilius who isn't bad."

'And that's not all.

'As Mathieu has plenty of time to spare, he drinks. But he drinks as an artist, by conviction, so he gets drunk regularly every evening. He is drunk, but he knows it. He knows it so well that every day he notes the exact degree of his inebriation. That is his main occupation; the chapel comes second.

'And he has invented—hear this and believe it or not—he has invented a *drunkometer*.

'This instrument does not actually exist but Mathieu's observations are as accurate as those of a mathematician.

'You'll constantly hear him say:

"I've been at 45 ever since Monday." Or: "I was between 52 and 58." Or: "I was at least 66 to 70." Or: "Well I'm damned, I thought I was around 50 and now I see I'm around 75!"

'He is never wrong.

'He asserts that he has never "got up to the hundred" but he admits himself that his observations cease to be accurate after 90, and so you cannot absolutely rely on what he says.

'When Mathieu acknowledges he has gone beyond 90, he is pretty drunk, you may depend upon it.

'On those occasions Mélie, his wife, another miracle of humankind, gets wild with him. She waits at the door when he comes home and screams:

"So there you are, you devil, you wretch, you drunken swine!"

'Then Mathieu, who no longer thinks it's funny, stands squarely up to her and says sternly:

"Shut up Mélie, I'm not talking about it now. Wait till tomorrow."

'If she carries on, he goes up to her and in an unsteady voice that shakes he says:

"Shut your mouth! I'm around 90. I've stopped counting. Watch out or I'll whack you!"

'So Mélie beats a retreat.

'If she tries to bring the subject up again next day he laughs in her face and replies:

"Enough said, it's all over. As long as I've not got up to the hundred there's no harm done. But if I go beyond that, word of honour, I'll allow you to tell me off!"

We had reached the top of the rise. The road disappeared into the beautiful forest of Roumare.

The autumn, the golds and crimsons of the marvellous autumn, blended with the last remaining green leaves, as if drops of melted sun had flowed out of the sky and into the dense wood.

We crossed Duclair and then, instead of continuing towards Jumièges, my friend turned into a small road that branched left through coppices.

And soon, from the top of a high hill, we again discovered the magnificent valley of the Seine and the snaking river stretching out below us.

On the right a very small building roofed with slates and surmounted by a tower no higher than a sunshade backed on to a pretty little house with green shutters covered in honeysuckle and roses.

We heard a shout:

'Friends!'

And Mathieu appeared in the doorway. He was 60 years old, thin, and sported a little beard and a wide white moustache.

My companion shook hands with him and introduced me; Mathieu invited us into the cool kitchen which doubled as a living room. He said:

'I don't have separate living quarters, monsieur. I don't like to be far away from my food. Pots and pans keep a fellow company.'

Then turning to my friend:

'Why've you come Thursday? You know very well it's my day for consultation with the Old Lady. I can't come out this afternoon.'

And, running to the door, he bellowed 'Mélie-e!' in a terrifying voice, which must have made the sailors on the ships going up and down the river in the valley below raise their heads.

There was no reply from Mélie.

Then Mathieu gave us a mischievous wink.

'She isn't pleased with me, you see, because yesterday I was around 90.'

My neighbour began to laugh:

'Around 90, Mathieu! However did you manage that?'

Mathieu replied:

'I'll tell you. Last year I only had twenty pecks of apricot apples, no more'n that. But they are the only thing you can use for cider. So I used up the lot and broached it yesterday. If you want to know what nectar is, that's it. You tell me what you think of it. I had old Polyte here. We had one drink and then another, but we couldn't quench our thirst—you'd be drinking till tomorrow if you wanted to do that. So in between glasses I was feeling a bit chilly in the stomach, so I says to Polyte: "What about a glass of brandy to warm us up?" He agrees. But brandy puts fire in your veins, so we had to go back to the cider. But then between the cold and the hot and the hot and the cold I realized that I was around 90. Polyte wasn't far off the hundred.'

The door opened. Mélie appeared and, without stopping to say hello, said:

'You drunken swine, you were both of you on the hundred.'

Then Mathieu got cross:

'Don't say that, Mélie, don't say that. I've never got up to the hundred.'

They gave us a delicious dinner outside, under two lime trees next to the little chapel of Our Lady of the Fat Belly, with a view of the vast landscape, and in tones of mockery but with moments of sudden credulity Mathieu told us tales of unlikely miracles.

We had drunk a great deal of this delectable cider, sweet and sparkling, cold and intoxicating, which he preferred to all other drinks, and there we were, straddling our chairs and puffing at our pipes when two women arrived.

They were old, bent and withered. After greeting us, they asked for Saint Blanc. Mathieu winked in our direction and answered:

'I'll go and get him.'

And he disappeared into his woodshed.

He was there for a good five minutes, but then came back looking very distressed. He raised his hands.

'I can't think where he's got to, I can't find him. But I'm sure I did have him.'

Then, cupping his hands, he bellowed again: 'Mélie!' From the back of the yard his wife replied:

'What's the matter?'

'Where's Saint Blanc gone? I can't find him in the woodshed!'

Then Mélie offered this explanation:

'Not that one that you used a week or two ago to stop up the hole in the rabbit hutch?'

Mathieu shuddered: 'By Jove it could be!'

Then he said to the women: 'Follow me!'

They did so. We followed too, suppressing our laughter with difficulty.

There indeed was Saint Blanc, shoved into the earth like an ordinary stake, spattered with mud and filth, providing a corner piece for the rabbit hutch.

As soon as they saw him the two women fell to their knees, crossed themselves and began to mutter prayers. But Mathieu rushed forward, saying: 'Wait a moment, you are in the dirt. I'll go and get you a straw pallet.'

He went to fetch the straw and made them a prayer mat. Then, contemplating his muddy saint, and no doubt fearing to be discredited for his transaction, he added:

'I'm just going to clean him up a bit for you.'

He took a bucket of water, a brush and began, with great vigour, cleaning the little wooden man, while the two old women carried on praying.

When he had finished, he added, 'Now he'll do.' And he returned to have another drink with us.

As he was putting the glass to his mouth he stopped, and in some embarrassment, said:

'I dunno, but when I put Saint Blanc with the rabbits I was sure he wouldn't make any more money. Nobody had asked for him for two years. But there you are, saints never go out of fashion.'

He took a drink and went on:

'C'm on, let's have another. Among friends you must never go less than 50, and we're only on 38 at the moment.'

The Voiceless

Christian Garcin

The sky is opaque and grey, but just below lights sparkle and the kaleidoscope of the Big Wheel flashes blue in the glass of the Hotel Bellevue and the *Northern Voice*. Soon it will snow. Pavements glisten, sledges slide and squeak, and children's cries light up the night. Tall, snow-powdered trees have taken possession of the square. Bells begin to peal. Something not unlike the warmth of childhood happiness is in the air. Emmanuel is standing still in the midst of a crowd of people. He's thinking about the end of the Capra film, *It's a Wonderful Life*, where James Stewart runs laughing in the snow through the streets of the small town he has come back to—at Christmas time, as it happens. It's the humanist argument for moderation, a tranquil, everyday sort of contentment, warm and domestic. Paradise lost. Here, as in the film, the shop fronts resemble theatre sets, the cold stings your face, lights are everywhere, the mist-spangled night comes slowly down and the pubs overflow with beer, smoke, and laughter.

Emmanuel has been staying in Lille for the last three days with Karla, whom he hasn't seen for six years—not since she left Marseille to go with her then boyfriend from whom she is now separated. A few months before that, Emmanuel and Karla had had a brief relationship, more of a sexual friendship than a real love affair. Then she left and the years passed. But about a month ago it crossed Emmanuel's mind that he might look up Karla again. He phoned her but she was out. At the precise moment he was leaving a garbled message on her answerphone saying he wanted to see her again, the postman was pushing a card from Karla through the letterbox, two storeys below, saying roughly what he had just said to her but in better-chosen words. The picture was a reproduction of a painting by Ary Scheffer, *The Dead Go Quickly*. Karla had written in tiny writing next to the title, 'We go slowly because we are alive.'

Emmanuel had already been to this town twenty years before, at a time when he was pursuing a girl he was madly in love with. She, for her part, wasn't in the least in love with him, and had firmly dissuaded him from following her, on the pretext, which he believed to be completely false, that she was already engaged to be married. He caught the first train to Paris, and then Lille, and after twenty-four hours with no sleep, and no food apart from a disgusting warm shish kebab and some bars of chocolate, managed to track her down. She was living in a small flat right at the top of a block of flats in a long dark street in the town centre, not far from a Chinese restaurant that had closed. It was summer and the weather was very hot—exceptionally so, he heard later—and the sun beat down. He found that odd, as the name Lille was more associated in his mind with greyness and cold. When she opened the door he could see behind her an indescribable mess, it smelled of rancid sweat, and all was steeped in a strangely charged, steamy, almost Mediterranean atmosphere. There on the doorstep she had told him to go, he had tried to stand his ground but her fiancé, a fair-haired guy with tattoos and wide, staring eyes, had threatened him with violence. He had talked loud and fast, in a thick accent that might have been Flemish, using words Emmanuel did not understand. So Emmanuel left, feeling rejected and removed from himself and the world around him, anxious and nervous in both body and mind. That was twenty years ago. Today he can't even recall the girl's name. Muffled up in his coat, in the middle of the crowd, he watches the big blue wheel slowly turning; there is a peal of bells, and he says to himself that with hindsight many affairs of the heart look too ambitious.

Karla lives alone with her three-year-old daughter and teaches English at Villeneuve d'Ascq. They have arranged to meet there on the last day of term, outside the Museum of Modern Art. Emmanuel has tried for three-quarters of an hour to extricate himself from the usual maze of industrial zones which have spread like a cancer and circumscribe all towns nowadays, suffocating them beneath their advertising logos, as mistletoe suffocates old trees. When he finally finds the museum, Karla has already gone inside and is waiting for him in the middle of a Barbara Kruger installation, alone in an immense forest of words written on walls, floor and ceiling, phrases such as: *Be like us, Speak like us, Think like us,* or *Love like us, Live like us, Die like us,* or even: *Everything that seems blind can see through you, Everything that seems deaf can hear you, Everything that seems dumb can speak through you.* 'Late as usual,' Karla said, kissing Emmanuel. She wore a green bandeau that kept her short black hair in place, framing her delicate, pale, oval face and emphasizing her bright violet eyes. 'And you're as beautiful as ever,' Emmanuel was on the point of saying, but a kind of diffidence held him back.

Karla lives in the old part of Lille, not very far from the place where the girl Emmanuel was in love with twenty years before had lived, the one whose name he cannot now recall. She lives at the back of the Cour des Mulets, in a narrow passage where there are weeds growing through the uneven paving, and piles of stone, made use of by a neighbouring sculptor now and again. A dark, silent cul-de-sac, exactly to Emmanuel's taste, with sprouting tufts of glossy, fleshy leaves lending the place a false air of the exotic. He hopes to stay there for a while, as long as Karla will let him. Almost opposite the entrance to the court-yard behind a faded sign, on which the words *Les Caves du Boucher* can still be discerned, broken-down tenements expose their blackened, disembowelled carcasses, at once fascinating and obscene. Standing still in the middle of the crowd that throngs around the big blue wheel, sur-rounded by laughter, chimes, and children's cries, Em-manuel remembers the ghostly silhouette he glimpsed just now in the pile of debris occupying the ground floor of one of these tenement blocks. There were charred beams, old stoves, up-ended cookers, mattresses, large torn canvas covers, hessian sacks full of rubble, lumps of breeze blocks, corrugated iron, empty bottles and cans, papers, filth, all scattered around among faded wallpaper, old tiles, a rickety staircase and some collapsed partitions. It's a sight that is poignant, insanitary, and infinitely sad, as he observed on arriving that first day at Karla's, just after the museum. There is something unsettling about seeing the inside of a house exposed like that on the outside, about being there in front of a world, so to speak, in negative, which holds centre stage instead of remaining behind the scenes, and displays the evidence of somebody's private life for all to see. It's like those flayed figures in anatomical plates where you can see their muscles, tendons, and intestines. I find that equally obscene. Karla said nothing, put her hand on Emmanuel's arm, and took him home with her.

So tonight, while Karla and her little girl are at a friend's house, Emmanuel is walking through the lighted streets, briefly immersing himself in the joyful, ringing Christmas hubbub, dominated by the big blue wheel. The people around him seem happy. He only glimpsed the silhouette out of the corner of his eye. It happened very quickly, just after he left Karla's place and emerged opposite the disembowelled block of flats. He thought he saw a shadowy figure slip between the rubble and the collapsed partitions, then climb the half-broken stairs leading to the two floors with their gaping, blackened windows. It was all dark, he is not very sure. Who can be living there? he wonders. Perhaps one of those new jailbirds who spend their days on their knees, heads bowed, in the streets full of shops overflowing with lighted boutiques. Could it be that chap—still quite young—who was on his knees yesterday on the frozen pavement in the Rue de Béthune, just under the four electronic hoardings advertising over and over again with an incessant, grating noise like a badly oiled pulley, washing machines, mobile telephones, and the latest Scorsese film.

It is starting to snow. Emmanuel moves away from the noisy, jolly square into the quieter streets. As he does so, he thinks he recognizes the one where, twenty years before, a young Flemish guy, probably drunk or slightly high, threatened him in the stifling heat of an attic room, under the approving gaze of a girl whose name he has forgotten. He arrives at the Rue des Bouchers, outside the ruined block of flats. Everything is dark and silent. Emmanuel hears the whisper of snowflakes falling around him. It makes him very happy. 'I don't quite know why,' he will say to Karla the next day, 'but I shut my eyes and had a feeling of pure well-being. Yes, I was out in the silence and the cold, surrounded by snowflakes opposite a sordid, half broken-down tenement building and yet my only feeling was a kind of quiet exaltation. A great sense of calm as well, which no doubt gave me the courage to climb the stairs, by the feeble light of my cigarette lighter, not knowing if they would give way under my weight. The first two steps were broken anyway and I stepped over them. The narrow, poky staircase squeaked a little. I put my head through the opening on the first floor, which was full of rusty mattresses and broken glass and open to the icy air. There was the ghost of a fireplace there, stuffed with paper and gnawed plastic. It didn't even look like a squat, or only one that had been abandoned a while back. I climbed up further. The second floor was almost habitable, the windows still had some panes of glass in them and the ceiling wasn't in too bad a state. There was a door leading into a very dark room. I didn't go in. Everywhere around me were deposits of frozen excrement, evidence of the use to which former squatters had put this place. A very acute, almost palpable, sensation of wretchedness suddenly caught me by the throat—it was like the reverse image of the quiet content that had filled me a few minutes before. At that moment I felt cruelly alone, naked and exposed,' Emmanuel will admit, 'and I felt like weeping.'

When Emmanuel returned, Karla was sleeping, as she did every night, beside her daughter. She insists on sleeping with her daughter, thus freeing up a room for him. Emmanuel understands and does not object. He goes to bed and quickly falls asleep. He knows that early in the morning Karla will come and join him before the little girl wakes. That's how it's been from the very first day, they have stayed together for part of the night, then she has left, and gone to sleep with her daughter, coming back early in the morning. They have resumed their relationship, in fact, exactly where they left off six years before—with perhaps just a little more tenderness. So towards seven,

Karla comes into Emmanuel's bed, rubs herself against him, kisses him on his eyelids. He caresses her face, her buttocks, her breasts. Karla's body is warm and flushed with desire in the mornings, her tongue soft and her fingers dextrous. She climbs on top of him and whispers words in his ear which he answers with an enigmatic smile. They laugh soundlessly and kiss each other's fingers, neck, belly, the inside of their thighs, they go on caressing each other for a long time. Their movements and their breath are in harmony. They learn how to make love again.

'We don't have a name for those people,' says Karla, half an hour later when they are sitting down to breakfast. The little girl, with intense concentration, is spooning down large amounts of cereal and milk. Today is fine, the sun is lighting up the room. Emmanuel has just been talking about the shadowy figure he glimpsed yesterday, and about his nocturnal expedition in the flats opposite. 'Here people usually call them tramps or SDFs,' says Karla, 'but they are all different. In English, or should I say, American,' she continues, 'there are three categories: *hobos*, the occasional or itinerant workers—there were swarms of them in the thirties, you find them in the books of Steinbeck and Dorothea Lange. Then there are *tramps*, who are also itinerant, but who don't work, they just drink. Here they migrate to the south at the beginning of winter. And finally there are the *homeguards*, the most numerous, the ones who booze and stay put: often they may have had jobs in the past, but have been ruthlessly rejected by the system. In Japan they are called *furosha*, "the men of the wave"; they are casualties of the free market and there are any amount of them. Sometimes *hobos* after a certain time become *tramps*, then end up becoming *homeguards*. The one you saw, if you did actually see someone, must have been one of them, someone who sits around boozing all day. There were a few of them in this block at one time. One room was apparently still habitable, with a sound floor, and ceiling in a decent state of repair and with windows that were watertight—I expect that was the one you didn't go into. The police drove them out one day, I don't know what happened to them. Do you realize,' she added, her voice rising, 'the buildings are abandoned, it's minus 10 at night and those guys don't even have the right to sleep there.'

She gets up abruptly, takes away the bowl from the little girl, who has finished, puts it in the sink and comes to sit back down again.

'I saw something else,' says Emmanuel. 'On one of the walls on the second floor was a sentence that was written yesterday. It was definitely the man I saw who wrote it.'

'A sentence?' says Karla. 'How do you know it was only written yesterday?'

'The writing looked as if someone had just done it,' says Emmanuel. 'I saw it just before I left. I put my cigarette lighter up close to it. And these words, rather puzzling: *The voiceless speak for you.* Below them was yesterday's date.'

The little girl has stayed at the table, staring at Emmanuel with her bright violet eyes like her mother's. He smiles at her. She drops her eyes, discomfited.

'*The voiceless speak for you,*' repeats Karla. 'What is that supposed to mean?' Suddenly her eyes widen, as though a thought has just struck her. 'That's funny,' she says. 'There was something similar written on the ceiling of the room I was in, something about the voiceless speaking for us, it was in the museum, do you remember, the day you arrived an hour late.'

'Three-quarters,' says Emmanuel. 'No, I don't remember.' And kisses her.

Later in the day, while Karla takes her daughter to the cinema, Emmanuel decides to go for a walk in the town. It is extremely cold. He dawdles a little in the pedestrian shopping streets which all look exactly the same whether in Lille, Marseille, Bordeaux, or Lyon, those paved streets with their interchangeable signs that have taken over the town centres throughout the country, while the industrial zones simultaneously encircle the suburbs. 'A perfect strategy,' Emmanuel says to himself. In another street he drinks a beer in the kind of pub where they insist on 'correct dress'. Everything about the place feels fake: a fake wood fire that works by gas, fake background music with badly mixed tracks, a fake blue-eyed waiter, fake, bored customers, one of whom, a fake blonde, no longer young, has a slightly lost look. He makes haste to finish his beer, to get out and go somewhere friendlier, not hard to find around there, and rejoin Karla.

He is on the point of paying, when he sees a tall, thin, stooped man in a woollen hat and a rather ragged dirty blue parka, with long tangled fair hair and a tow-coloured beard, chewing a Havana cigar, walking along the pavement. His breath is escaping out of his mouth like steam. He suddenly stops, raises his arms and claw-like hands to heaven and utters a few curses, before going on his way. Emmanuel cannot tell exactly what he is saying, but thinks he can make out the words *for you*, or perhaps *for us*. His heart starts to beat faster, he thinks it could be him. The man stops again, and again throws his arms up in the air but this time he stands stock still without uttering a word, 'just as if he could feel me looking at him through the window of the pub,' says Emmanuel to himself. Then the man turns his head and scowls at him, pointing a finger at him and muttering something. Then he points a finger at himself, speaks another word or two, and forces his features into a toothless smile before saying something else. Emmanuel is embarrassed but returns his stare. He believes he recognizes him. 'It's him,' he thinks. 'I'm almost sure it's him. He has the same eyes as the Flemish drunk of twenty years ago, up in Agathe's flat, that's it, I've remembered her name, she was beautiful, she was called Agathe and she wanted to be an actress.' The chap in the parka goes away shouting something. Emmanuel opens the door but a taxi is accelerating and he can't hear anything. He does not dare to follow. Why follow him anyway? He watches him disappear, then leaves in the opposite direction.

'Do you like this town?' asks Karla.

It's evening, the little girl is asleep in her bedroom. Emmanuel and Karla have a few hours ahead of them, part of the night before she goes to join her daughter. They are sitting on the sofa drinking brandy.

'Hard to tell, I don't know it very well,' says Emmanuel. 'But I suppose so. I love all northern towns.'

'Ah,' she says.

'And then I like you being here,' he adds.

Karla smiles and says nothing. There is a silence. Karla gets up, chooses a CD, and the voice of Laurie Anderson floats out into the room.

'I went back to the abandoned building,' says Emmanuel. 'The writing was still there, but the date was rubbed out and underneath was today's. The guy came back in the course of the day. That's weird, isn't it?'

Karla hesitates.

'I don't know,' she says finally. 'What difference does it make?'

She comes and snuggles up next to him.

'Isn't it nice like this?' she asks.

Emmanuel does not answer immediately. He is thinking about the man he saw that afternoon. When he pointed at him through the pub window and then pointed to himself and grimaced, Emmanuel thought he had understood him to say: *For you*, then *For me*, and then, enunciating the words carefully: THE SAME.

'Yes,' he says finally. 'It is nice like this.'

Karla takes hold of his hand, strokes his fingers.

'When are you leaving?'

She isn't looking at him. Emmanuel lightly kisses her eyes and then her lips.

'I don't know if I am leaving,' he says.

The Garden of Illusions

Pierre Mac Orlan
for Jean Sallas

Hidden here and there along the river-bank, some of whose bushes along the edge trail newly-broken branches in the tranquil water, four field-guns are pointing their single barrels to the sky.

These four battle-boats have turned the river and the countryside of Picardy into something resembling an exotic landscape in Tonkin. The yellow-skinned gunners in their national *salakos* or blue cloth berets complete this impression.

The guns are motionless, under roofs of quivering leaves. On the armoured deck behind the first turret, striped blue and white jerseys are drying in the sun.

A foreman in blue overalls is fishing with a line, watching the furrows on the water. Bare-footed sailors watch a flight of wild ducks pass over the marshes in a V-formation.

By the side of the road along the canal the men of an infantry battalion have stacked arms, and laid their packs on the ground. They are in the ditch, overwhelmed by the stifling heat, having a bite to eat or lying flat out on the dusty tufts of grass, observing with great interest the activities of a busy beetle.

It is the hour when the whole battalion lives, breathes, bathes in the blessed light, and thinks of nothing.

Behind us the quarries are swarming with workers; they look like slaves performing some religious rite. One might think they are building a temple where the helmeted Bambara, whose duty it is to make the lorries turn left, will go and deposit his useless magic charms.

We are thinking of nothing. The grasses are full of tiny delicate things that have suddenly become important. To us stretched out on the warm ground, this simple umbel of hemlock looks like an umbrella pine, whose clear silhouette cuts us off neatly from the question: Why are we here?

This need to remove oneself from present reality, from both future and past, I find it in all my comrades. They have all become contemplative. Each man's soul, according to his particular sensibility, slows down and falls asleep in front of a flower, or while reading an old newspaper that has been read and reread many times, personal columns included. Reading in this case has no more importance than a physical exercise. Since for the time being we are unable to kill anything, we do our best to kill time.

It is a time of perversity, when everything that lives disturbs the torpid harmony of minds relaxing. That house over there, still intact, is manifestly shocking. We enjoy the idea of the first shell piercing its unblemished wall; that new roof with red tiles deserves all it gets. And that stupid bird should go off and sing somewhere else; a bullet in his feathers would do him good. We flail with sticks at the slender stems of the timothy grass or the exuberant poppies.

It will be a long break. We shall not leave until nightfall, for the road we are travelling in order to take up our new position goes over a rise from where the enemy can see us.

In front of us the village of X— offers the familiar shape of systematic destruction. A colourless pile of debris lies where the old town was, the ancient one that was there before the war. On the hillside a strange new town appears to have risen up out of the earth, its roads and buildings grouped into variegated terraces.

This shimmering city was born of fantastical dreams. It is the creature of war, it will never evoke reminiscences of a literary kind.

A strange little town whose plank houses merge with the unevennesses and colours and accidents of the landscape. It is an ever-changing mosaic where among the leaves and lumps of clay your eyes eventually manage to make out some spots of pink, orange, green, yellow, and blue, so that they stand out and one object is set off against another.

We are trying to make sense of an enormous cubist picture, which stretches right down as far as the canal, whose water, not yet painted in, gives us a *point de repère*, and allows the mind and the classically educated eye a place to rest.

This artificial and cunning decor looks like a picture constructed out of illogical fragments, like pieces of a jigsaw puzzle cut out in such a way that the person doing it will be deceived as to the normal form of the objects he has to reconstitute.

That is the excessively personal background of modern warfare, its peculiar style that means you cannot compare it with other wars.

In the midst of this strange and fantastic picture, which seems not to fit together and whose secret rules are like a key we are not in possession of, individuality crumbles away. The armed man is no more than one fragment in the chaotic frieze, and for that reason you never hear any anecdotes celebrating the sometimes prodigious strength of character of an individual; or they get lost, as they must, in this setting so hostile to the displaying of such strength.

Yes, it is difficult to sketch out one of those pleasant little anecdotes so beloved of people who are totally ignorant of war, in this setting that does not make any sense, where a cannon may resemble a flowering apple tree as readily as it does a mossy rock, or where an officer on watch is himself dressed in a coat which gives him the appearance of a heap of bricks, a hawthorn tree covered in bees, or even a lump of mud.

In this curious transformation of nature, you do well to keep your nerve. The setting reminds you of nothing so much as certain terrible periods in prehistory. A diplodocus on the rampage looks very like a self-important 420. Whereas a *drachen*, when not in operation, rather resembles the silhouette of a crouching glyptodon. Iguanadons and stegosauruses, the heavy artillery of the jurassic landscape.

The soul of an immense machine hovers over this fusion of disparate elements. Here man is a living molecule that does not even have the capacity to reproduce itself by fission. One telephone call will be enough to let loose the horror of all this latent machinery and make of the earth on this evolving planet a pretty curious hell, strewn with putrid geysers and foul-smelling craters.

The creaking of the hoists, the softly throbbing motors, a sound like wings, like bees, shifting the heavy gun-carriers into a Petit Trianon of artificial foliage; and already our ears are hurt by the sharp blasts of the whistle, the blood rushes to our swollen temples, our heads are spinning with a worrying charge of energy...

'Packs on!'

The twilight makes the landscape ugly; its false gaiety was only hanging by a thread: a single ray of sunshine.

We shoulder our packs. Our companies form up. Some groups go ahead. I can see the bugler from the fifth battalion.

'Hey, you coming with us?'

We march along roads paved with rose-coloured bricks towards pulverized houses that have been made famous by the latest communiqués. We are not especially eaten up with curiosity. We are more preoccupied with knowing for sure if getting across the river and the canal will be a bad few minutes or not.

No, no, all will be well. The liaison sergeants say so. Confidence is restored and swiftly those few words warm our hearts like a powerful cordial. A few of us are tempted to be over-optimistic.

'Oh it's always the same. If you listen to those chaps from the nth regiment, we'll all be blown sky-high when we arrive at C— It's no worse there than anywhere else. If you ask me we are better off in the front than the second line. And in any case we can't do anything here. Where do you think we'd attack? They'll get more men in to hold the line and it'll happen to the right or the left of us. The only comparison with that sector, mate, would be Souchez— *the Shooters' Trench, Hollow Way,* and the *Bridge Sap,* that one went on for ever. You been there?'

The conversation goes to and fro. I note it in passing. It's the kind of conversation you hear before each attack when everyone comforts himself the best he can.

As for me, I swear we will attack. The liaison officers never get the signs wrong and the signs have been increasing all around us for several days. Will we get through?

Rue de l'Évangile

Marcel Aymé

In the La Chapelle area of Paris lived a poor Arab by the
name of Abd el Martin. He was called Abdel for short
or Crouïa, or Arbi, or Scumbag or sometimes Fleabag,
because he did indeed have fleas.

The northern end of La Chapelle is hemmed in by bare
walls that hide factories, warehouses, railway lines, gasometers, dirty trains, and towering locomotives. The
smoke from the rail networks of the East and North
mingling with the smoke from the factories blackened
the jerry-built tenements, and the never busy roads
resemble run-down provincial streets marooned in a
wasteland of rust and coal. This is a literary landscape
where a sensitive walker, hearing the trains whistle in the

grimy fog, might be surprised to find himself praying that life won't last for ever.

Abdel lived in the Rue des Roses at the bottom of a cul-de-sac in between two oozing, grimy tenements, on three damp stone steps, which led down to a blocked doorway, protected by a roof of rotting wood. Neighbours who came back late at night would sometimes go as far as the end of the alley and take a good look at him in the flame of their lighters, as he slept in the old army greatcoat which he wore day and night. The more inventive among them would prod him with a foot, saying: 'Arrouah arrouah, chouïa chouïa', perhaps with the fraternal sense that they were bringing themselves down to his level. He would respond with the little hoarse squeak that seems to be the basis of the Arabic language and off they would go, content.

In the morning, at the sound of the first dirty water gushing over the cobbles in the cul-de-sac, he would rise, remove his army coat and put it back on again. Having thus performed his toilet, he would go shuffling off down the Rue des Roses. The housewives who rose earliest and went shopping before they left for the factory would look at him in disgust and quite openly make hurtful remarks. After he had gleaned a few leftovers from the top of the bins he would stay a good while outside the Café du Destin and pass the time watching men at the bar breakfasting on coffee or a white bordeaux. Customers would nod in his direction and mutter to each other: 'Look, there's the Crouïa', in aggrieved surprise that he was still alive, when so many good men, useful to their families and the Republic, gave up the ghost every day. Now and then Monsieur Alceste, the owner of Le Destin, would tap on the window with a coin, beckoning him in. 'This'll make you laugh,' he'd say to the clientele. Filling a bowl with vinegar, he showed Abdel a twenty-cent coin and, with a wink, offered him the deal. Abdel never hesitated but swallowed it in one gulp. 'That would be the death of any normal man,' the owner would observe, as everyone cried out in amazement, and nearly always he added: 'But from a scientific point of view it's interesting enough.' Madame Alceste, the owner's wife, who wasn't interested in curiosities of science, considered it a sheer waste of money and merchandise and, with a shrug of her shoulders, pulled a sour face behind the counter. Still a young woman, she was small and stout, with the nipples of her large, low bosom showing through beneath her bright silk blouse. The shadow of a dark moustache lent her plump face an air of passion and mystery.

Apart from the times when he was invited to drink vinegar, Abdel had one more chance of being allowed into Le Destin. At the slack time when the workers had just left his bar, the patron, sweeping the café floor, would sometimes be weighed down by the vanity of the human condition, and, looking through his window, would view the world as a barren pavement on which Abdel was doing an interesting job. He would open the door and say: 'Arbi, bring your fleas in here.' Once again Madame Alceste, sitting at the back of the café, would shrug her shoulders, yet without lifting her nose from the cinema magazine, dreaming she was Mae West or sometimes, on a good day, Greta Garbo. Leaning on his broom-handle, watching Abdel drink a tepid coffee, the patron might go so far as to meditate aloud:

'When you think about it,' he'd say, 'human beings are not worth much. Take you, for instance. What are you? Scum. Where do you come from? Nobody knows. What use are you? I was talking to my barber about it once and that's exactly what we said, the government ought not to allow vermin like you in the country, especially in a city like Paris, the heart of France. I'm not against foreigners, quite the opposite, but I reckon there are limits, all the same. First, if you were to vanish—shot or whatever—who would know? Nobody. I might say to Madame Alceste: "Hey, we don't see that Crouïa who used to drink vinegar around here any more?" And that would be that. And I would have forgotten all about you in a fortnight, no doubt about it. That's a sure proof that you are worth less than nothing.'

While he was being talked to in this fashion, Abdel gazed at the *patron's* wife with eyes bright with passion. He was sorry he couldn't rape her; for, being a gentle and unassuming sort of person, it never crossed his mind that he might get anywhere with her by paying her attentions or compliments. Quite often at night on his three damp steps, he would dream about her; she was like a voluptuous pillow that imparted some tenderness and human comfort to his hard bed of stone and sometimes his nearest neighbours were surprised at the softness of his moaning. But not even his happiest dreams disposed him to ask any more from life; and even as he devoured Madame Alceste with his eyes, he never expected her to raise her own to him with a burning passion. The only jealousy he felt was over the glamorous figures he saw on the pages of the cinema magazines who, it seemed to him, removed the patron's wife into a world even more remote than the Café du Destin.

On leaving the café, Abdel went along to the little Place Hébert where he made another important stop. Standing on the pavement at the end of the Rue des Roses, he looked at a place, often deserted, on the far side of the crossroads, the Rue de l'Évangile disappearing into the distance between two high, blank walls bordering on the right the sunken eastern railway lines and on the left the huge area of gasometers whose high and monstrous casings seemed to hang over the road as if to crush it. Abdel viewed this steep-sided street devoid of houses and pedestrians with fear and curiosity. Several times already he had ventured down it, but, overcome by panic, and feeling the world withdrawing from him, he had been obliged to turn back. A few hundred metres from the Place Hébert it bore to the right and seemed to go on for ever between its two bare walls, until it was lost. In the grey, smoky light of morning it looked unreal, like the exit into a gloomy infinity or a desolate corridor into some inaccessible paradise. In actual fact he knew it led nowhere but when he looked at it from the square and saw a lorry emerge from it, he wished he could have said something, stopped the driver and asked 'Where have you come from?'

All day, trailing round the *quartier*, Abdel dreamed of the Destin owner's wife and the deserted Rue de l'Évangile. During the morning in the market of the Rue de la Guadeloupe, where he was on the lookout for food and purses; in the afternoon on the benches in the Boulevard de la Chapelle; and in the light of the shop windows as he brushed up against the girls touting for custom, and felt he had entered a forbidden garden, the same images came to haunt him. And in the evening, when it was time to go to sleep, he imagined he could still see the stocky figure of Madame Alceste melt away into the distance in an empty, dangerous street.

One Sunday morning, while her husband was sweeping the floor in Le Destin, Madame Alceste was reading in *Votre Cinéma* the plot of a moving film. Its hero was a handsome young man who had joined the Foreign Legion and had a romantic tattoo on his chest. Though his prowess went unacknowledged by his warrant officer, he fought like a lion and always had a dreamy look about him which made women think of sex. The wife of a famous scientist, who had come to Africa to study the habits of grasshoppers, falls for the simple soldier and they make love in the warm, scented evenings. In the end the lover dies heroically in the middle of nowhere, saving the famous scientist's life and his wife climbs up on to the terrace of a Moorish house to sing a heart-rending song into the night. The title of the film was *Mon Légionnaire*. Madame Alceste, her eyes damp and her bosom stirred by love and heroism, did not even hear her husband shout to Abdel le Crouïa through the half-open door. She was looking hungrily at the photograph of the hero who, haggard and in rags, but radiant with passion, was rushing headlong into danger after a day's march without water in the desert. At the same time her heart contracted with anger and regret at the thought that her café proprietor husband would never go to Africa to study the habits of the grasshopper. Still young, and with her soul unsatisfied, she must renounce all thoughts of burning sands, unbridled passions, and comfortable remorse. And yet she felt that she, as well as any other woman, might have made the soldier's body burn with the mysteries of love and sung of his death in couplets brimming with emotion.

Abdel was drinking a cup of coffee and the *patron* was holding forth to him about the different categories into which he would have placed the human species if, instead of being the owner of a café, he had been God. His omnipotence, however, did not render him any more indulgent towards the Arab, to whom he unequivocally assigned a place in the lowest category.

'If I were God, the fact I knew you personally wouldn't make any difference. I know your sort and I wouldn't hesitate for one minute...'

Suddenly he broke off and leaning towards this wretch of a human being, scrutinized him with new attention. Then, surprised and indignant, he jumped back and cried:

'Hey, Madame Alceste, have you seen this little swine's eyes? Have you seen the way he dares to look at you?'

These words, which meant no more to Abdel than the ones that had preceded them, did not distract him from his contemplation. Raising her eyes, Madame Alceste met the wild look of the Arab and her heart began to beat more quickly. Leaning on the bar, in his old army greatcoat, with his tanned, dirty face, he seemed to her a soldier burnt by the African sun and bearing the glorious stains of combat in the folds of his soiled uniform. She had found the heroic figure from *Votre Cinéma* there before her in real life, and recognized deep in his warm eyes the male, savage desire that she had just been secretly invoking.

'Louse!!' cried the *patron*. 'So that's how he honours the laws of hospitality! Well I'll have that coffee back for a start!'

At the *patron's* threatening face and his tone of voice Abdel felt he had done something wrong and, putting the cup down, looked towards the door. Madame Alceste, her face pale, had risen and was clutching her bosom with both hands. A nagging sense of the domestic realities prevented her from intervening and giving way to her passion. Her husband was threatening the Arab with his broom and pushing him roughly towards the door.

'I'll show you. I'll teach you respect. Get out, you scum! And don't come back here again!'

Madame Alceste, bruised and cast down, was incapable of making any move. But when through the café window she saw the Arab disappearing down the Rue des Roses faintly then she murmured:

'Mon légionnaire...'

As he made his way towards the Place Hébert, Abdel was thinking about the change in the *patron's* attitude and couldn't understand what had happened to him. He was certain he had behaved quite normally with regard to his hosts at Le Destin. He did not in the least suspect that his constantly looking at Madame Alceste might have offended the *patron*. He never imagined for a moment that his desire for a woman so far beyond his reach might lift him out of his lowly state and draw upon himself the attentions of the powers that be at Le Destin. And Madame Alceste's turmoil, even had it been more obvious, would still have escaped him. In any case he had a very simple explanation for his fall from grace: that they just did not like him any more and the reasons for this were less important than the consequences. The ban which had just been placed upon him brought with it an upsetting of the usual order of things and it was with a sinking heart that Abdel gradually realized this. It meant the end of those long stops outside Monsieur Alceste's café and of the coffees drunk at the counter while he observed from over his cup the soft outlines of the *patron's* wife. As he whiled away the time through the long days, his visits to Le Destin were his main source of dreams, and on the rare occasions when he went so far as to wonder about the future, his tomorrows were always situated in the context of the Alcestes and their café.

Arriving at the square he stopped as usual and gathered his thoughts for a moment. It seemed to him that his life was suddenly empty. He did not feel like wandering round as he had on other days. The *quartier* bored him. As a rule he felt there was always some kind of connection with Le Destin as he walked. Whenever he stole a piece of fruit or a pot of jam from a stall he always felt protected by the distant presence of Monsieur Alceste.

Now when he raised his eyes, he saw in front of him the Rue de l'Évangile, its bleak emptiness vanishing into a dirty smog. It beckoned to him like the road to forgetfulness. He wanted to bury himself in it, and, turning his back on the *quartier* of La Chapelle once and for all, set off to discover a new world. He walked once round the square and stopped where the street began. In front of him there stretched out an endless, silent wasteland, constrained between high grey walls and deep in secrets. At his back he could hear the gentle hum of life on the quiet crossroads. Men went laughing into a café on the small square and he thought he could detect the smell of sawdust and vermouth. A sweet nostalgia held him fast between the two pavements. He felt too heavy to explore the unknown. For one moment he looked at the blue plaque that bore the name of the street, hesitated once more, and then, retracing his steps, made his way back towards the market.

He walked briskly, as though pursued by dangerous temptations, but gradually the day-to-day preoccupations came back and calmed him. As he entered the market hall, he struck lucky. Glancing round, he saw first a woman in poor clothes carrying a newborn baby in her arms. She put down her purse and her string bag next to her on a pile of empty crates to administer a smack to another, whining child who was clinging to her skirts. Abdel had no compunction whatsoever and preferred preying on poor people, knowing from experience that the well-nourished react more dangerously. He put his hand on the purse, slipped it quietly into one of his greatcoat pockets and managed to get to the exit without any trouble. He went down the Rue Pajol towards the Boulevard de la Chapelle, taking his time and counting the money in the purse, about ten francs. He was neither hungry nor thirsty, only eager to rest and escape from his worries. Having wandered along the boulevard for a little while, he entered a café that had a poor appearance. Half a dozen young men who normally went there on Sundays were sitting at a table drinking and talking about their bikes. A woman with platinum blonde hair, no longer young, stood at the window smiling at passers-by. She was also smiling at the young men in the café but without any thought of money, rather in a sociable, eager-to-please sort of way.

The owner greeted Abdel with a scowl. On a Sunday morning the arrival of such a dirty individual made a bad impression. Abdel dared not sit down but went and settled himself in front of the counter. The girl behind the bar asked him in a tone of suspicion what he wanted. He showed her his money in the palm of his hand, but in reply to her questions could make only hoarse and abrupt little noises. The owner followed the exchanges with hostility.

'Okay, let him have a coffee and then clear off,' he said in a very loud voice so that the clients would understand perfectly well that this was an accidental intrusion. 'A fine specimen,' he added.

The platinum blonde began to laugh and looked at the young men. They broke off their conversation to give the Arab the once-over. Their curiosity was not unkind, but his army greatcoat amused them. Abdel, fearing laughter was about to erupt, was already contemplating leaving before he had finished his coffee. One young man got up and walked round him with an air of admiration, saying as he pointed to the filthy greatcoat full of holes:

'When you've worn out your suit a bit, be kind enough to pass it on to me, will you?'

Everybody roared with laughter. The platinum blonde left her observation post and came up to the bar with the intention of asking Abdel for the address of his tailor. Amid the noise of the laughter and the pointed remarks, she couldn't make herself heard, which upset her. As he was making his way to the door, she went to cut off his retreat, in the hope of repeating her attempt to be funny. He tried to avoid her and accidentally bumped against her and stepped on her foot. She was furious, and began insulting him, calling him a shit, a thief, a witless sick bastard. She even went out after him to shower him with more insults and there in the middle of the pavement cried out that he was flea-ridden and poxy, and more besides. Passers-by stopped, to get a better view of the man who had deserved such cruel truths. But what affected Abdel more deeply than the insults, of which he had only taken in their intent, was to discover two Arabs amongst those who had stopped. These Arabs, who were decently dressed and might almost be described as elegant, accompanied two women of the *quartier*, no doubt their wives, for one was holding by the hand a little curly-headed girl with a dark skin. They looked at him in silent, dignified disapproval and in their eyes he saw not so much mockery as censure. Abdel felt an acute regret at having hesitated to go down the Rue de l'Évangile and his one thought now was to leave a world so decidedly hostile.

He had already walked two hundred metres down the Rue de l'Évangile and had passed the bend, so that he could no longer see the tall gasometers that, from a distance, seemed to dominate the view. The street was reduced to nothing but its two high walls, and at the far end vanished in the fog. In none of his previous attempts had he been as far as this. And moreover, when he set out there on weekdays, he encountered lorries and there would be some comfort in their presence, furtive though it was. On Sundays the road was dead, not a soul about. There was no sign of life and whatever was substantial, man-made—the walls and the pavement—was so absolutely geometrical as to lack all human connection. From time to time Abdel could hear the whistle of a locomotive, sad as the cry of a bird in an autumn field. At each step he could feel the city, the whole world, withdrawing from him. He was aware of the area of La Chapelle only as an unsteadiness. His memories were fragmenting, becoming more distant, and parts of his most recent past were already obscure to him. He tried to think about where he was going, but he had insufficient resources to imagine it, even confusedly. He had fewer and fewer points of contact. Even the name of the street, which he had never been able to make out on the blue plaque, was an unknown quantity. It seemed to him that he was nowhere and floating in a void. His head swam. He raised his eyes to the sky to try to escape the stranglehold of the walls, but the sky was low and weighed on him like a coffin lid.

Abdel stopped in the middle of the road and looked down at his feet and his greatcoat for a moment, to regain some sense of his own identity. It did him good to see his feet. One of his toes was poking out of a hole in his shoe and he amused himself by wiggling it. It was like meeting an old friend. Being able to wiggle that dirty, muddy toe reminded him how sweet life was. For a minute his memory opened up a little. The game made him remember a few of his nightmares, rather like the one he was living through now. In those dreams he was carried away into the solitude of an inhuman chaos, where shapeless mountains pressed upon him from all sides; then, waking with a start, the hard, sticky surface of his three stone steps was an inexpressible delight, as if happiness had begun at the first frontiers of life and all the chance encounters in the world could but add to, or take away from it, unimportant details.

Abdel finally tired of his toes and began to be worried once more. He felt dispirited, his head felt stiff and his legs were weak. Before he set off again he glanced over his shoulder and saw that the fog had closed off the road behind him. Unsure whether to retrace his steps or go on, he turned and turned until he lost all sense of direction. Between its two high walls the street ended in fog in both directions. Terrified, and now quite resolved to go back, he looked from right to left but could not guess which way. At last, pretending an assurance he did not feel, he chose the right, and quickened his step. Soon he doubted he had made the correct choice and ran back the other way. For several minutes he went back and forth, always at a run and always afraid he might go deeper into the unknown. Then fatigue and the fear of getting even more lost halted him. He was anxious to know how long he had been wandering like that in the Rue de l'Évangile but had no idea. All notion of time eluded him and he was afraid of being forgotten by the world of the living. He saw death in the image of an eternal, blind wavering between two directions. He began to examine the walls, looking for a human sign to fix his mind on. Taking care not to go too far, he proceeded slowly, like a prisoner exploring his prison. Crossing the road to have a good look at the other wall he had a nasty shock. There before him, in a careful hand in large capital letters in charcoal on the stone, were the words: 'Hang Casimir!' Abdel could not read, but the meaning of the words would not have made him any happier. The indecipherable message was nevertheless a message from the world of the living. He could not take his eyes off it. His universe re-formed itself around those large black capitals. Through Casimir he could see the *quartier* of La Chapelle, its grey, faded streets, its provincial food market, its run-down shops, its damp cafés. Le Destin stood out in a singular fashion and the mysterious figure of Madame Alceste appeared, dreamlike, in one of the capital letters. More ancient memories gradually revived in him: sunny lands, family, cattle, ploughing, brightly-coloured villages, black towns, a prison, forgotten friends.

Momentarily reassured by these images, he thought he might discover other and more precisely eloquent writings that would allow him to get a sense of where he was going, but his search was haphazard and he quickly lost sight of the two words scrawled in charcoal. Scared he might not find them again, he started to turn round and round, then to run in various directions. Finally then finding himself by chance face to face with the large black letters again, he stayed with them. He crouched down by the wall and pondered the secret script. When he looked at them for some time, he found that each group of letters acquired a face. But the word 'Casimir' pleased him more than the other one did. A delicate charm arose from the grouping of its mysterious characters and dulled his anxiety.

The noise of an engine, still some way off, made him jump. As he got up, a car came out of the fog on his right. It was going at a rapid pace. Abdel got off the pavement and began shouting and gesticulating. Fearing to run over a madman or believing he was being warned of some danger, the driver slowed down, stopped a few metres away and looked questioningly at him. Abdel's move had been spontaneous. He had not had time to think in advance and in any case conversation would have been difficult. In his confusion he pointed to the inscription. The driver, apparently unaffected by this kind of message, shrugged his shoulders and drove off. For a second Abdel stood where he was; then he started to run after the car, shouting, with a vague feeling that he would be saved if he kept up with it. For twenty yards or so he almost succeeded in keeping pace. The car speeded up and he increased his speed too. But the distance which separated them was widening rapidly. Soon the car had disappeared into the fog, but Abdel did not let up. He could still hear the purr of the engine, almost as reassuring as a visible presence. With his head down and teeth clenched, he ran blindly, straining towards a goal he could not even imagine. Finally he stopped, out of breath. There was a vast murmuring in his ears. He thought he had come upon a large and unknown city and found himself back on the little Place Hébert. Two women he had noticed before as he passed through were still gossiping at the door of a lodging house. His trip into the Rue de l'Évangile had lasted somewhat less than a quarter of an hour.

In the evening in the Rue des Roses at the bottom of the cul-de-sac Abdel returned to his three stone steps with feelings of affection and gratitude. He took a long time to fall asleep because all the things he had to be glad about were going through his mind. In the first moments of sleep he thought he heard a light footfall approaching.

Someone came down the first step and a foot hit against his knee. He pulled himself up on to his elbow. In the cul-de-sac the night was thick and darker still in the hole where he lived. A female form, soft and ample, leaned over him. Feverish hands, in their impatience, unbuttoned his greatcoat. He did not dare move. The woman pressed her body against his, slipped a hand under his shirt and, putting her mouth to his ear, whispered 'Mon légionnaire, mon légionnaire!' She repeated it several times, with a sort of insistent passion, as if she were knocking in a nail: 'Mon légionnaire.' Abdel held his breath, the better to appreciate this ardent whisper. All the sweetness of his recovered city came down to him that night on his bed of stone.

Half an hour later the woman rose, uttering the same mysterious words with a sigh and in a more languid voice. The Arab tried make out the figure departing so quickly up the cobbles of the cul-de-sac, but the night was dark. He went back to bed and fell at once into a deep sleep.

When he awoke next morning, huddled up in his great-coat, he thought for a long time about his female visitor. Knowing no other woman but Madame Alceste, his first thought was of her. He found the idea that she should come looking for him absurd, but it was pleasant and convenient to give the unknown woman the features of a woman he had desired. Leaving the cul-de-sac he avoided passing in front of the Café du Destin, partly because of his quarrel with Monsieur Alceste but especially so as not to court bad luck. The memory of the night was enough to fuel his daytime reveries. Through the streets of the *quartier* of La Chapelle he searched in a happy nervousness for the face of love and found it without difficulty in the features of Madame Alceste. When night came he was more and more anxious in case his lover did not return.

He got back to his retreat towards nine, as usual. He thought he might go and watch out for her at the end of the cul-de-sac but a vague sense of the respect due to apparitions kept him from doing any such thing. The unknown woman arrived punctually towards a quarter to ten. She was carrying a blanket that she spread out on the stone and took away with her when she left. Their lovemaking was just as it had been the night before and again Abdel fell asleep that night without having seen the face of the woman who was making love to him. Nor did he try to force a revelation, far preferring to imagine her with Madame Alceste's features.

On the third evening the unknown woman was punctual but she took less time about what she did and she showed a certain nervousness. She no longer planted her lips on the Arab's ear and called him 'Mon légionnaire' but confined herself to issuing her orders and giving him sharp injunctions. It worried him and he feared for the future. The next day he woke rather later than usual. Coming out from the cul-de-sac he saw Monsieur Alceste musing with the broom in his hand on the doorstep of Le Destin, and he withdrew in the opposite direction.

The owner had recognized the Arab. He watched him for a moment then spat into the middle of the road and went back inside his café. Madame Alceste was reading the latest number of *Votre Cinéma* and as she read, her cheeks flushed with wave after wave of colour. The film that interested her now was set in high society. The son of a big businessman was playing tennis with an orphan girl from an excellent family. They got married at Saint-Philippe-du-Roule after many vicissitudes, all of a decent nature, which threw into relief the delicacy of their feelings and the elegance of their dress.

Behind his counter Monsieur Alceste was moving bottles around to clean a shelf. He left off what he was doing, put his cloth down and scratched his head with both hands. Glancing then at his wife he remarked:

'So are you scratching as well?'

Madame Alceste, hand halfway to her head, looked up from her magazine, blushed violently, and replied:

'Yes, I am. I can't understand it...'

'My head has been itching for two days and this morning it's driving me crazy. I couldn't speak to you just now, but while I was serving the customers I saw a flea on the counter. Lucky nobody but me saw it, but when I think...'

For a minute the husband and wife scratched freely and unembarrassedly.

'As soon as I saw that Arab wandering round in his greatcoat I thought: I wonder if he's the one who brought them in...'

'Just what I was going to say,' said Madame Alceste.

'Sunday morning he was in the café, remember. I was stupid enough to call him in.'

'Ah, you see now, I was right not to want him in here.'

'So you were,' said her husband, 'but I thought I'd taken enough precautions all the same. The truth is, in any case, the government never should allow such creatures in the *quartier*. If I've said it once, I've said it a hundred times.'

'That's true,' said Madame Alceste. 'We are not being protected properly.'

They resumed their scratching. On the page of *Votre Cinéma* the wife's eyes lingered over the slim figure of a young man in a suit. Raising her head she said to her husband, 'Why don't you speak to Monsieur Ernest about it?'

'That's not a bad idea...I'll try and see him this afternoon.'

The two inspectors entered the cul-de-sac at an early hour of the morning. One was a young man wearing a soft felt hat cocked on one side and a raincoat whose belt was casually, and becomingly, knotted round his waist. The other, Monsieur Ernest, was turned out in a more traditional fashion. He was thickset, with a moustache, the shoulders of a prize fighter and enormous calves that made a distinct curve on his trouser legs; he wore a bowler hat and black overcoat cut in the style of a civil servant.

Abdel, who had spent a dreadful night vainly waiting for the unknown woman, was still dozing on his three stone steps. Monsieur Ernest flashed his torch on him and contemplated the pile of rags with an experienced air.

'Amazing,' he said to his companion. 'When I tell Pondeur that he won't believe me.'

He tapped the sleeping man's shoulder with his foot and shouted at him to get up. Scarcely taking time to stretch, Abdel emerged from his hole. Despite the half light, which did not allow him to make out their faces, he at once realized who it was he was dealing with. Monsieur Ernest examined him carefully with his torch and concluded, with contempt:

'Scum, a piece of shit... Work for the fur trade rather than for us.'

When Abdel, as a mark of protest, made some squeaky sounds, he pushed him with his finger in disgust and said:

'Keep your trap shut, sweetheart. You can talk at the station.'

The resigned Abdel followed the younger of the two inspectors. As they came out of the cul-de-sac he glanced in the direction of Le Destin. The café owners were on their doorstep. The owner watched with an expression of sympathy that was only slightly tinged with irony. Madame Alceste's face was hard and austere.

His eyelids still heavy with sleep, the Arab walked along between his two captors, head bowed and paying no attention to the familiar surroundings of the Rue des Roses. He only felt a vague anxiety about his present circumstances and it was all mixed in with his troubles of the night and the fatigue arising from his lack of sleep. The policemen were talking to each other calmly about their work and their colleagues, and did not pay him much attention. Picking up a vagrant was an everyday sort of job, of no interest to them.

At that early hour, the Rue de l'Évangile was still quiet and empty. There were no lorries passing. Arriving at the Place Hébert, Abdel automatically looked that way. A thin line of mist was still sticking to the pavement, hanging like cotton wool between the two distinct grey walls. At the bend the tall gasometers seemed to watch over the silence like gigantic armoured fortresses. Abdel took a step back and ran across the square. He was convinced that once he had started down the Rue de l'Évangile, he would be safe from the city and the world and nobody would ever again be able to find him. A few metres from his goal the police recaptured him. There was no struggle. Abdel gave himself up without resisting. Monsieur Ernest grunted, threatening him with the back of his huge hairy hand:

'That's enough, you little rat.'

Two railway workers on their way to the Rue des Roses passed in front of the group and one of them laughed and said to the other:

'Look, there's the Crouïa going on his holidays!'

At the entrance to the Rue Pajol Abdel glanced back for the last time, his shoulders twitched and it seemed he might try to escape again. Monsieur Ernest, with an agility that one would not have expected from a man of his age and stoutness, landed him a couple of powerful, well-aimed kicks on the back of his greatcoat, which made him cry out. On the pavement an old woman walking her dog made a movement of pity and protest.

'You have to, with these animals,' said the inspector. 'They don't understand anything else.'

Light Souls

Stéphane Émond

He is standing outside the small station of Sainte-Méné-
hould among all those shapes thrown into relief by the sun
at their backs, like an entire regiment taking its ease;
straighter than the others, almost rigidly upright in his
greatcoat, with his black armband on the left arm, his *képi*
pulled firmly down over his head, booted and spurred, he
is waiting for his brother, or more precisely, the remains of
his young brother who has been killed in the Argonne, for
the greater glory of France, as it says in the photos in
L'Illustration. There are twenty to thirty of them, all
officers or sub-lieutenants, Italians and French all mixed
up, together forming one single regiment, a rough sort of
cohort—their alliance will seem rather surprising in a

little less than three decades from now—yet here they are, together, fixed in one attitude, patient, thoughtful. They hear the train, whose engine needs oiling, snorting its way slowly up the hill from Biesme. On 31 July 1914, in the Paris evening papers and reprinted the following day, was the notice: 'A certain number of citizens living in Paris and profoundly attached to France have decided to form a corps of volunteers who, in the event of armed conflict, will put themselves at the disposal of the Ministry of War in order to support the action of our armed forces.' Next day at the Café du Globe, three thousand Italians assembled. In one week, eleven thousand Italian citizens sign up at the volunteer headquarters. In the autumn Peppino, Costante, Ricciotti, and Bruno Garibaldi were in the Argonne. In accordance with French military law, they were stripped of the decorations affixed to their green tunics after their daring exploits and feats of arms in Greece and in the Balkans. The memory of those wars of stones and rocks was not a distant one, but this time round it was mud that awaited them, the mud that old d'Annunzio was glorifying almost at the same time as they were fighting. Man hunts man in the woods and thickets; exposed, vulnerable, he goes to ground like a rabbit. Whilst in the grand apartments of the Via Cavour in Rome the children of absent fathers are running excitedly round the Christmas tree, the latter have forgotten it's

Christmas and are preparing to attack near the old priory of La Chalade. Beneath their green tunics their red shirts are bright and easily spotted, but they have kept them on despite the orders of the French sergeant major. Man hunts man, and though a thousand have come from the Abruzzi or Puglia or Genoa, Pavia or Salerno, to walk along the ancient Roman road, very few will go back home. Fifty would perish that very night.

At around four in the afternoon, Bruno is hit in the left arm by the first bullet, which hardly hurts him at all. Propped against a tree and yet protected, he is hit full in the chest by the second, then by a blast of four more. The young soldier with him, petrified more with fear than cold, hears him say:

'Give my love to my father and brothers.'

Until nightfall, the three brothers look for their youngest in the thickets, in the woods, in the plantations. When they see him sitting slumped against a tree as though asleep, they are prevented from approaching by the guns. Stuck there waiting they think they see him stir, raise his head just slightly.

'He moved,' said his twin, 'I saw him.' Unable to do anything, so near he could reach out and touch his hand—and yet so far off. Above them the sky—not yet one of nature's casualties—makes wavy clouds and sends down a fine, icy rain. Night has come, they attempt to get

nearer, but the crackle of branches underfoot is dangerous. So they wait and try to sleep. When day breaks, the
body has fallen on its side, they can actually see the face
with its eyes wide open. At midday the waves in the sky
drift out as far as the horizon and to the distant roar of the
forest. The tunnel they are digging will allow them to
reach him. At nightfall they are fifteen metres away and
at midnight a young volunteer corporal goes crawling off
to fetch Bruno. Centimetre by centimetre he brings him
back to his brothers, using him as a shield, feeling the head
swing on his shoulders from side to side like a pendulum.
He takes an hour to cross those fifty metres, his mouth
filled with earth, his eyelids stuck together, and blue
with cold.

Christmas came and went two weeks ago, and his body
was at rest in La Forestière, from where he was exhumed,
so on this nearly spring day—the air is warm—his brother
is waiting for him, standing up straight in his boots
outside the small station. The station-master comes to
warn them of the imminent arrival of the train. He throws
away his cigarette, crushes it with his boot, one of his
spurs grates, he fingers his moustache. He goes towards
the door of the waiting room; all the shapes, cut flat by the
sun's shadow-play, make way for him as he goes forward
and follow him, leaving the square deserted. The French
and Italian flags on the roof seem not to be moving. On

the other side of the tracks, a shepherd, as though suspended up on his hill, is grazing his sheep. Shading his eyes against the sun, he watches the train as it emerges from the tunnel and the brakes are applied with a great clanking and rattling. When it comes to a halt, he turns his eyes to the station clock which says six o'clock. Across four or five railway tracks, the weeds growing here and there among the ballast, are the military, who salute the coffin carried on the shoulders of four Italian soldiers. At the sight of the coffin, he makes the sign of the cross and whistles to his two dogs, who begin to gather in the flock. In the distance beyond the forest, he hears the sound of firing and the world turned upside down, a world full of souls, so very light and so many of them, they make a soft fluttering sound as they pass . . .

House in the Woods

Stéphane Émond

Is it not enough to watch the newborn leave so soon? Why do the oldest have to leave too? She had had to grieve over two of the eleven that life had given her. The oldest, who had left home very early, had scarcely known the youngest. The last baby arrived just after she had celebrated her forty-sixth birthday.

She has been working since dawn. The days are large and hot now, with a beautiful brightness falling gently, that warms her body through the day and places a shawl around her by night. The forester's house they live in can be seen from a long way off when approaching from the road. It's handy for seeing people coming. You have time to put a comb through your hair, take your apron off or hide from visitors should they be unwelcome. When the long line of children trail home from school, the older ones leading at the front and the little ones dragging behind, she watches out for them and prepares bread and butter that they devour when they reach the house.

She can hear the shouts of the woodcutters working in the forest; one of them is singing; the wind carries their voices right up to the house. That's where he must have gone this morning. He had to oversee the progress of the felling on the slopes. If she stood on the edge of the well, she might almost be able to see him with his axe in his hand or measuring the length of a tree-trunk. She knows he will come down quite soon and leave for the fields, stopping on the way to see what he has snared.

The last letter from her eldest is dated three weeks ago. That's not like him, he writes every two or three days. It makes her very anxious, for the news from the front isn't good. Under the assault of the German artillery, the whole front is retreating from east to west. In his last letter he wrote that he had three days' leave, and said he was in good spirits and would be celebrating his birthday with his cousin in Commercy. The parcel had arrived safely:

'Every spoonful of jam makes me feel very happy. It must have been very hot and sunny for the fruit to be so sweet and firm. Be sure to tell the little ones and the big ones I'll be home soon. If it's warm enough we'll have a great bathing trip to the river. Don't forget that if the dog is barking and fussing, the best way of calming her down is to make up a good basin of milk sprinkled with a bit of sugar. She just loves that. Give her a pat from me. I send you hugs and am thinking of you a lot.'

The little dog is asleep in her kennel, with her head in the morning sun. The mother looks at her, envying her animal indifference. For the last few nights she has been woken by an ache in the pit of her stomach, always at the same time in the middle of the night, so she gets up, goes for a little walk outside, goes up and checks that the little ones haven't thrown off their blankets, looks at the clock and, if it is not too late, goes back to bed. Last night the whole field in front of the house was lit up and the path along the edge of the forest looked like one long, un-broken wave.

The pain has not left her since daybreak. She is just finishing picking vegetables when she sees him coming down the edge of the plantation, his game-bag slung across his shoulders and carrying a hare by its ears. She stands up to ease the pain in her stomach. As she straight-ens herself and turns towards the village, she sees, in the distance, a figure leave the road and make its way with a calm and measured tread up the lane. At first she cannot identify his massive form with any certainty, but then, little by little, she recognizes him. She knows that the man making his way down past the wood can also see that figure. And when the mayor comes nearer, takes off his hat and places his hand on the gate, she lets out a great wail and runs out towards the man whose footsteps have slowed down as he descends. Her wail echoes to the four corners of the forest around the house. In the distance the woodcutters raise their heads. The little dog jumps up, leaves her kennel and, leaping over the fence, runs down the lane, barking furiously.

Nos choucroutes

L'authenticité avec un grand A.
Choucroute et charcuterie nous viennent directement des meilleurs faise
Cuites à point. Parfumées à coeur. Elles se sont mises à "neuf" pour satis
votre goût et votre appétit.

houcroute aux quatre saveurs . . . .
ucisses de Francfort, Montbéliard, Nuremberg, Munichoise.

houcroute brasserie . . . .
ucisses de Francfort, Montbéliard, lard, saucisson à l'ail

houcroute paysanne . . . .
ucisses de Francfort, Montbéliard, Munichoise, Nuremberg, lard

Choucroute en ribotte . . . .
etit salé, carré de porc, 1/2 jarreton, sauce aux échalotes

Choucroute de Maître . . . .
n jambonneau entier demi-sel cuit à l'os

Choucroute strasbourgeoise 1
aucisses de Francfort, Montbéliard, Nuremberg, Munichoise, lard, carré de po

Choucroute de la Taverne 2
aucisses de Francfort, Montbéliard, Munichoise, Nuremberg, lard,
carré de porc et demi jambonneau (servie en deux fois)

Choucroute du ramoneur 1
une cuisse de canard confit, saucisses de Francfort, Nuremberg, Montbéliard, la

Choucroute de la mer 25
lieu fumé, escalope de saumon frais, rascasse, langoustines, crevettes,
moules, avec une sauce beurre blanc. «Une création de la Taverne, l'accord parfait»

Choucroute bien garnie,
plaisir garanti !

The Phantom of Rainbow Street

Didier Daeninckx

I sat on the waterfront, my legs dangling over the edge, and put down my sandwich, scarcely even touched, upon the uneven paving stones. A seagull swooped by and hovered, as if it knew I wasn't hungry, and I watched his rapid reflection mirrored in the calm water. The crumbs I threw on to the surface drew him down. For a little while I watched the bird eat his silent meal. Then I rose and crossed the great sluice gate, a sort of long enclosed bridge, slung across the banks of the Ill. The passage was dark, interspersed at regular intervals by cells with heavy iron grilles imprisoning the damaged cathedral statues, a winged angel with its smiling ox-head, for example.

I bought my newspaper from an itinerant street-seller in the Quartier-Blanc, who was propping up the tower that also served as a urinal. The fire hadn't made the front page, only two small columns on page 6: 'Fire in the Rue de l'Arc-en-ciel, one dead.' The identity of the victim did not figure in the account. The anonymous journalist had pushed discretion to the point of ignoring my presence on the scene when the drama took place.

My singed eyebrows told a different story. But when I think about it, he was right. There was no reason why I should be in the Rue de l'Arc-en-ciel in Strasbourg that October night! In the normal run of things I should have been in Paris in the warm, putting the finishing touches to an article on Godin's phalanstery. But he could not know about the winds of madness that regularly blew through the offices of my accursed rag. Especially on Sunday evenings.

'Jean-Pierre, you're off to Strasbourg!'

The chief editor stood before me. He had taken care to look the part: open-necked shirt, rolled-up sleeves, loosened tie, hunted expression with beads of sweat caused by genuine anxiety. I looked up from my stuff on Guise, my pen poised, in the middle of a word.

'And what the hell am I supposed to do in Strasbourg?'

He adopted a yet more tragic expression.

'I can't move from here...But there's a scoop to be had. They've just uncovered some murals by Arp and Van Doesburg in the Ricard saloons...'

I threw down my pen.

'You've got the wrong man! Go and ask Philippe or Alain, that's their kind of thing. Lascaux's not my scene!'

'That's not funny. They're slaving away on the inauguration of the Hôtel Salé. They've got to revise the whole of Picasso. I can't hold them back. There's a lot of publicity for the galleries in their article. Take a return ticket. Anyway, one day in Strasbourg isn't the end of the world, the town's not so bad. And as for the grub...'

The memory of its gastronomic delights brought tears to his eyes. I agreed.

As soon as I arrived I hurried along to the Ricard rooms in the Place Kléber, and found a notice on the brass plate: 'Closed Mondays.' I would have to stay an extra day. The documentation service of my newspaper had not been able to provide me with the tiniest photo of the wretched murals.

I had to make do with the photocopy of a biographical notice of Hans Arp, 'painter-designer-sculptor-poet, born in Strasbourg in 1886', which made mention of the Aubette wall-paintings. According to the document, in 1926 a patron had asked Arp and Van Doesburg, an architect companion of Mondrian, to do the architecture and design the interior of a vast leisure complex comprising a cinema, night-club, saloons, bar, billiards, and exhibition hall. The result was the largest ensemble of abstract art in the world. The whole of Europe visited it between 1927 and 1939, then just Germany, but at the Liberation nothing was left! The disappearance of the joint work of painter-sculptor and architect was put down to the army of occupation in its struggle against degenerate art.

The Indian summer had bypassed the town. Over by the model trains passers-by were warming themselves at the chestnut vendors' grills. I sacrificed to the ritual and went back up the Rue des Grandes-Arcades, burning my fingers on the way.

The museum of modern art occupied part of the site of the old customs buildings. I set myself to finding out where the section devoted to Hans Arp was. In vain: it had just been put into store in order to make room for a Duchamp exhibition! The conservator handed me a leaflet.

'I'm sorry, but we're only putting it back in January. Have a look in the Galerie Alsacienne, the address is on this leaflet, they've also got some documents on l'Aubette.'

I went back through the pedestrianized streets to the Place du Château, finishing my chestnuts on the way. The cathedral was sprouting pieces of metal tubing upon which workmen in silhouette were hard at work. In places the façade was recovering its original rose colour.

The Arp corner of the Galerie Alsacienne possessed two sculptures, a few drawings, and a plan of the saloon of l'Aubette, the 'Five o'clock', accompanied by black-and-white photos of certain murals. Huge compositions, which one could imagine in colour, covered the walls of the rooms where the volumes were waiting to be sorted. Painted areas extended from walls to floors to ceilings, the stairs, the partitions, the radiators, everything fitting together in the overall design. I tried to take photos of the exhibition displays without being very hopeful of success. When I got back to the foyer a crowd had formed in the entrance. The woman behind the desk, a large lady with glasses and a gentle face, looked at me and addressed me in Alsacien.

I raised my shoulders in a gesture of apology and then asked:

'Do you have a catalogue of the Aubette murals?'

She looked surprised. Surprised and sorry.

'There used to be a little booklet on Van Doesburg, but we've run out. If you go up to the library on the floor above they could at least show you a copy.'

The librarian looked thirty years younger and thirty kilos lighter than her colleague. The archivist of one's dreams: refined, blonde, and friendly. And it was with a melting charm that she announced:

'The collection is in the process of being computerized. The acquisitions from the last ten years are in cardboard boxes. There are nearly fifty thousand unclassified volumes. Are you from Paris?'

I nodded.

'You'd easily be able to find that catalogue in the Bibliothèque Nationale.'

She moistened her lips with the tip of her tongue. I took in her words of advice without batting an eyelid. Her voice stopped me in my tracks as I was leaving.

'I'll have a look and see if there is anything available. Give me a ring tomorrow morning. Ask for me. My name is Annie.'

When I left they were getting ready to close the museum. Night was falling. Scraps of mist were rising from the Ill, enveloping the pillars of Saint Madeleine's bridge. I dived into a brasserie near the Place Gutenberg and, with my mug of Grüber beer before me, tried to reflect on my wasted day. Shortly after eight, four students from the regional study centre, employees of the BNP, or so I gathered from their conversation, sat down at my table. They ordered *tête de veau* and eyed my sauerkraut as they guzzled their gelatinous dish. I was halted on my way back to the hotel by the neon lights of the UCG cinema.

Rampling offering her body and Serrault wearing a tie, caressing her... The film did not, however, fulfil the somewhat louche promise of the poster.

The exit from the cinema was at the back of the building and I got lost in a labyrinth of streets which were all completely new to me. The occasional passers-by I came across hurried on their way; they were wrapped up so tightly in their between-season's clothes, they might as well have been shut up inside their own houses. I decided to make straight for the water, on the edge of the old town, but soon, like going back in time, I felt that my walk no longer needed an aim. My route was deflected by a sign, by the position of a street, an evocative name. Wandering from one to the other at random I wound up in the Rue de l'Arc-en-ciel, which I continued down after emerging from the Rue des Pucelles. It was a narrow, winding street, with buildings from various periods. A modern residence which occupied the corner of the street was backed on to by an old decrepit building with flaking shutters. A tiny untended garden led to some stairs with a rusty balustrade. I don't know why this house caught my attention. The sadness of it? That feeling of being abandoned? Or the movement I thought I saw behind the curtains on the first floor? In any case what I did was take cover in the darkness of a stone porch nearby. I stayed there a quarter of an hour, my eyes fixed on the grey façade, getting colder and colder. Suddenly the front door above the steps opened a fraction. Then, for several minutes, nothing happened. I was just preparing to leave my shelter when the door opened a bit more. The broken figure of an old man appeared, looking all around him. He went down the stairs, muffling the noise made by his footsteps, and crossed the little garden. He went along the pavement a yard or two, and then stopped in front of a restaurant whose curtains were closed. I saw him plunge his arm into the dustbins, his head raised like some crazy periscope above the stinking rubbish. He trotted back to his cave, clutching a few unspecified leftovers to his chest. The door silently closed. The whole thing had taken no longer than a minute and I was ready to believe I had dreamed it, had not a chicken drumstick, with a bit of chicken still on it, cracked under my shoe when I passed this strange habitation.

The Ricard rooms opened to the public at ten. A young Indian girl with a tattoo on her forehead was passing a vacuum cleaner over the stair carpet. On the first floor behind the bar, a guy of about 30, small, with narrow shoulders, was occupied in putting the glasses away according to size. On the walls, which were covered in cream-coloured hessian, there was an exhibition of work by local artists: paintings of leaves, metal reliefs, embroideries... I leaned on the bar.

'We're not serving at the moment. Not till eleven o'clock.'

'I've not come for a drink... I'm doing an article on the murals of l'Aubette. Do you know where they are?'

He pointed to the back of the room where a series of hideously discordant tapestries hung.

'There are some over there, for sure, and round the rest of the room!'

My eyes opened wide.

'You don't mean to tell me I've come all this way for that shit?'

'They're awful, that's what I think, too. The murals are behind the hessian. They were drilling in that corner for the electricity and the workmen discovered them. There's a false wall protecting them.'

I went over to the wall and raised one of the tapestries. A clumsy mend in the cloth showed where they had been drilling.

'If I understand you correctly, the Germans were not so barbaric as people claim. All they did was cover the pictures up.'

The barman joined me.

'Not even that! They didn't have any hand in it. When they arrived in 1940 Hans Arp's work was already invisible. The owners of l'Aubette had sold the business in 1938 and their successors weren't great lovers of modern art. They're the ones who boarded them up.'

His patriotism, which lurked below the surface, was satisfied when he added:

'That's definitely what saved those murals. I'm certain that if the Germans had spotted them there would be nothing left!'

He went back behind the bar and started to line up his glasses again.

'Can I peek behind the cloth? Just to get some idea of what they are like?'

'Impossible. Everything's been filled in again. We are waiting for a team from the Ministry of Culture. What you could do is go and have a look next door at Flunch, they inherited part of the rooms and basements. That was where the nightclubs were.'

The young Indian girl was winding in the extension lead when I left the Ricard saloon. The Flunch restaurant occupied the whole ground floor of the right wing of l'Aubette. At the counter the waitress was turning out her trays of breakfast. I explained what I had come for, being interrupted all the while by orders for coffee, chocolate, espressos. She called 'someone from the management' who piloted me through stock rooms, damp recesses, places for dustbins. This 'someone' halted between two blackened pillars.

'There you are, it's at the back, on the wall.'

'Is there a light?'

He pressed several times with his forefinger on a wrecked light switch.

'No, it must be the mains.'

I crossed the room, whose floor was littered with stones, pieces of wood and paper, by the light of my cigarette lighter. The 'mural' consisted of half a square metre of wrapping paper stuck on the wall on which some local artist had drawn a few traditional characters. So that was what Flunch thought the work of Hans Arp was like!

'Have you found it?'

I made do with a nod. A chef met us on our return journey.

'Were you looking for the murals?'

'Yes, why?'

He shrugged.

'There's nothing here any more. They were all burned at least twenty years ago.'

I still had the library catalogues to go through. I made a stop at La Fringale, a fast-food restaurant which turned out dishes adapted to Alsatian gastronomy, and ordered a doughnut. I remembered what the girl in the gallery had suggested. I squeezed into a phone booth on the place Kléber and dialled the number of the museum.

'Could I speak to Annie?'

I was treated to several bars of Mozart, then interrupted by the voice of the archivist.

'Yes?'

'I came yesterday about the paintings in l'Aubette.'

'You are in luck, I have found some documents which might interest you.'

I could hear her riffling through her papers, opening a drawer.

'Here we are. The decor was reconstituted in 1955 on the campus of the University of Caracas in Venezuela. I have a file with photographs. Is that any good?'

I promised to come round in the afternoon and then hung up, feeling rather disconsolate. I was beginning to get seriously fed up with these invisible murals that no one here seemed to give a damn about.

My hotel was just nearby, in the Rue du 22 Novembre. I was tempted to go and get my things and head back to Paris. I don't know what pretext stopped me: the rendez-vous with the blonde at the museum, or the furtive vision I had seen the night before.

Immersing myself in the books on the municipal shelves taught me very little: the name of the sponsors of l'Aubette, the Horn brothers. An enterprising couple who had made their mark on Strasbourg. It was they who had built the road where my temporary abode stood. They gave it the name of November 22 to commemorate the collapse of the Strasbourg soviet in 1918, when the Breton regiments arrived!

I had a beer in a student café. The alcohol slowly did its work. To stretch my legs a bit and rid myself of the stiffness which was invading my muscles, I set off to wander the streets. I was not surprised, suddenly, to recognize the façades of the Rue des Juifs. I branched right towards the Place Saint-Étienne and found the Rue de l'Arc-en-ciel again. A few people were crowding into the restaurants clustered further up the street, this side of the crossroads. The abandoned house looked exactly the same, both sinister and poignant. As I got nearer I noticed that the door, which didn't shut properly, had made a neat fan shape as it scraped over the dust on the steps.

A couple came out of the house next door. The woman was carrying a tiny dog under her arm. The animal's head was invisible in her fur coat. I accosted them, and pointed to the grey house:

'Excuse me, but do you know who lives here?'

The man paused. He looked up at the front of the house.

'Nobody very much, I reckon. We've just moved in. You'd better ask at the corner café. They've been there for donkeys' years!'

There was roast chicken on the menu. I sat down and ate, waiting for the moment when I might be able to get the inside story from the patron. As is usual, the opportunity arose when he came and leaned over my table to work out the bill.

'You've been living in this area for a while I understand?'

'You can't always trust what people say, but they are not telling fibs. I was born in this house fifty-five years ago and have never left it! That'll be 63 francs, with the coffee.'

He held out the bill to me.

'So you must know the old guy who sleeps in the grey house further up the street?'

He frowned and shook his head.

'Are you talking about that half-ruined shack?'

I nodded silently.

'Never been an old chap there! It's been empty for six months ever since the old Kagen woman kicked the bucket...'

'You sure?'

'Positive! She lived on her own after the war. Funny woman, grumpy and reserved as they come! She lost her husband when she was young, mind. Forty years without a man, your nerves must be bloody awful.'

He gave me a long look; I put a note next to the bill.

'What are you after, exactly?'

I had the disagreeable impression that he took me for someone looking for a bargain, sent by an estate agent.

'Nothing. I thought I had saw an old chap come out of the house surreptitiously, like a thief.'

He returned to the bar to sort out the change. I followed him.

'Must be a tramp who's hit on a good place. There are more and more of them in town. They have to shelter as soon as it starts to get nippy!'

Back at the hotel, I called the newspaper. The editor-in-chief began shouting at me.

'What the hell are you up to? You might give some sign of life. I need your article for tomorrow night. We've advertised it. How far have you got with it?'

'Nowhere! The murals are boarded up, the museums have placed the remainder in storage and the documentation is awaiting classification. They are putting all the catalogues on line, just for fun. As for the library, we only have access to the shelves. The place is in the process of being reorganized. Having said that, I've got an important lead on a remake of the murals in Caracas. Do I have the go-ahead?'

'If you've got the ready, by all means! But before you do, make a detour via the paper and deliver twenty pages of copy—okay?'

I stretched out on my bed, my writing block in hand, and had a go at my article. 'A Masterpiece of Modern Art.' A banal sort of title that I crossed out in order to replace it, daringly, with: 'The Sistine Chapel of Modern Art.' That also ended up being crossed out. By nightfall I hadn't crossed out anything else. But nor had I written anything either. All I had done was miss my rendezvous with the young blonde from the Alsatian gallery!

I had a meal brought to my room and swallowed it automatically while I watched a German programme on the telly. Outside the mists from the Ill were gradually invading the streets, making the silhouettes disappear. I waited until half past eleven to go out. I walked across the town, taking my time. The grey house produced in me the same impression of desolation mingled with nostalgia as it had the day before. I took up my observation post in the corner of the porch. I couldn't discern the least sign of life for the first hour, which I spent absolutely motionless, analysing in detail the progressive numbing and stiffening of my body. I almost fell asleep, but the sound of the door being scraped open jerkily on the cement wakened my senses. There was the old man in the doorway, legs bent, arms folded, back arched. He looked all round to see that the coast was clear, then scurried across to the dustbins outside the restaurant. I took advantage of his hasty trip to cross the road and climb the steps. I pulled open the door and went into a dark room where there was a strong smell of decomposing matter.

I was preparing to go in further when the door shut behind me. The old man was facing me; a fear identical to the fear that was making my heart beat so fast could be seen in his face. He remained frozen for some seconds and then dashed to the stairs on the left-hand side of the room, howling:

'No, you won't get me. Never . . . never . . . '

I rushed after him. The steps of the staircase were spattered with rubbish and excrement, and my feet slipped on it. I heard him raging around in the rooms above.

'I don't want to harm you. I'm a friend.'

I had reached the landing. I picked up a newspaper, shook off the filth clinging to it and rolled it up like a torch. The damp paper lit reluctantly, spitting out little blue and green flames. I made my way towards the access to the loft, holding my makeshift torch in front of my face. As I passed the fourth door, the madman rose behind me. He was rendered hideous by the moving shadows created by the flickering of the flames. Fascinated by the brightness of his eyes, I did not notice the bayonet he was holding in both hands. He started shouting, a meaningless roar, and charged at me with the weapon pointing at my chest. I just managed to get out of his way, but his shoulder caught me and made me drop my torch. He was already coming back at me. I made my escape by leaping down the stairs and found myself on the pavement again, gasping for breath. The old guy had not followed me. I drew breath, leaning against the front of the house. A passer-by shouted at me.

'Hey, there's a fire up there!'

I looked up. The windows on the first floor were sending out a reddish glow and smoke was forcing its way out between the tiles.

'Quick, call the fire brigade! There's somebody in that house!'

I rushed back to the building and re-entered the down-stairs room. The fire had dispelled the foul smell. I made for the stairs. The top steps were already alight. The heat of the inferno forced me back. The firemen managed to control the fire before it reached the ground floor. They found the charred body of the old man, his hard-cinder hands grasping the handle of a bayonet. Thanks to the papers kept in the kitchen drawers the police established that it was without any doubt the body of Roger Kagen, husband of the so-called widow who had died six months before. Like 132,000 men from Alsace he had been con-scripted into the Wehrmacht in 1942. Like thousands of such men he had been put into an SS regiment. Dozens of them had found themselves in the *Das Reich* division and the destiny of Roger Kagen had been sealed at Oradour-sur-Glane, 10 June 1944, outside a church in flames.

Since his clandestine return forty years previously he had lived as a recluse in his house in the Rue de l'Arc-en-ciel in the heart of Strasbourg; it was only the death of his companion which had obliged him to return to the world of the living.

The journalist from *L'Alsace libérée* assigned to 'news in brief' waited for the man from the rescue unit to finish examining my burns. He drew me to one side.

'I hear you are a journalist from Paris.' (He nodded towards the smoking house.) 'Not very nice all that ... And here we don't really believe it's necessary to dredge up all that shit yet again ...'

I rubbed my eyebrows to get rid of the singed hairs. I felt very old.

'You do as you please. It's your patch. Perhaps you'll be surprised to learn that I am here for l'Aubette and only that.'

His eyes widened, very likely he doubted whether I was of sound mind.

I folded my newspaper, threw a last glance at the gulls flying above the Petite-France, and went back to the station. In the train to Paris I got out my pad and reread, through all the crossings-out, my attempts at a headline.

Suddenly I tore out the page, and then, in my most careful handwriting, I inscribed the letters of the best title of all: 'The Phantom of Rainbow Street.'

The Saviours of the White Wine

René Bazin

'What a princess!' he exclaimed.

And he pointed through the window at the slopes opposite, covered in vines.

'But what a whore as well!' he added. 'What a lot of people she's ruined, great and small! But now we are beginning to trust her again. The whole of France is replanting. This district, mentioned in Rabelais, reputed for its white wine since the fourteenth century, inhabited by what amounted to a caste of wine growers, abundant in wine presses, grape thieves, drunkards, and thrushes, phylloxera ravaged it worse than the war, or two or three successive invasions: a whole people almost completely vanished and at least a third of the land left waste. From my living room here I saw the slopes all covered in ferns for more than ten years. Not one plough furrowed them, not one mattock sent its metallic sound to rattle my windows. Today you can see the poles in regular lines, like hatching, in all the fields where vines were cultivated before 1870. Indeed, I believe they have planted beyond the old borders. The same goes for all the neighbouring districts. A new race of wine growers has sprung up, more knowledgeable, better equipped, less conscientious than the last. They add sugar, monsieur! But the phenomenon is none the less worthy of historical record. The vineyards of France have reconstituted themselves. An enormous gamble has been taken on the vine. If you want some idea of the amount of money we are risking, I can tell you that each hectare replanted costs me more than three thousand francs. And I am only one of numerous risk-takers. And I'll even admit that I have put all the enthusiasm, all the energy I have left, into this venture.'

The man who received me thus was an old doctor from the Saumur region, who, having exercised his profession for some while in the town, had done what people scarcely ever do nowadays and retired to the country. He had the portliness, the fresh complexion, and the twinkling eyes of the traditional wine grower. A quiff of white hair combed from right to left and ending in a kiss curl above his ear told me plainly that he had been around at the time of the July Monarchy. On the walls naively papered to look like marble hung some pale, neat engravings by Calamatta after the pencil portraits by Ingres of my friend's father and of three women in his family.

'Yes,' he went on, 'I am passionate about this experiment in wine growing, on which I believe the fortune of France depends. And I believe we shall win. One of our worst enemies is dead and the other is ailing.'

'To whom do you refer?'

'The first is the carelessness which centuries of easy profit had induced in our old wine growers. When they had to graft on the American vine, nobody knew how. Lacking specialists, they asked ordinary gardeners who were used to grafting pears and apricots. But what a mistake, Monsieur! What profound differences there are in these skills, which may seem so alike! We who were preaching by example and were the first to replant, we have learnt that to our cost. How many *rupestris* and *riparia* I lost through not knowing which soil was suitable to each, through lack of care and intelligent attention! Today, thanks to the schools of grafting, thanks to the competitions set up each year by the prefects in one district or another, there is now not a single canton which does not possess its Doctors of Viticulture, simple peasants become Master Grafters—don't you think that title has rather an *ancien régime* ring to it?—who show off their diplomas with pride, and also know how to prune the new vines, fertilize them, and see that they survive. Add to that the great progress we have made in the development of the presses, the methods of vinification and the treatment of the wine, and you will understand what I meant by my assertion that one of the enemies of viticulture is dead. The wine grower is armed now. But he has other extremely dangerous enemies.'

'Namely?'

The old wine-growing doctor smiled so that his thin lips widened and at that moment he looked exactly like the son or the nephew of the beautiful ladies in Calamatta's engravings.

'Ah, what enemies our French vine has made and still has, Monsieur, not to speak of the ingratitude she has aroused! Many of my colleagues have been unjust towards the one who first gave us alcohol, but who alone can cure us of it. They are unaware of its supremely important role in French history. They do not wish to acknowledge that French blood is neither Latin nor Celtic nor Germanic but is quite simply made out of crimson grapes and that is why it is so fervent. At one time I thought these people would carry the day. I who am now, despite my age, so full of hope, fifteen years or so ago I believed that the white wine, our real treasure—the most inimitable, the liveliest, wittiest, loveliest of all our wines, the one whose vapours vanish and are forgotten soonest—was about to die out under the insults of our medical practitioners. People no longer bought those casks of the wonderful wine we made from the old vines that today have been burned and have vanished, or at least the middle classes mistrusted it and made a detour to avoid our hillsides. If we had not had . . .'

The servant opened the door of the living room where this conversation was taking place and said:

'Monsieur, the Commissioners of the Société are here.'

'Very well, I am coming.'

He rose, and beckoning to me, said:

'Come with me, you shall meet the saviours of the white wine.'

We soon found ourselves in the cool vaults in my host's cellar with three peasants in their Sunday suits, shaven, serious, and somewhat self-important. They had the fresh complexion of peasants from the valley of the Loire. They were most certainly persons of note, and greeted us with a condescending nod.

The oldest of them said: 'We have come to buy, if you have something worth buying.'

His voice proved that my friend's cellar was not the first that the commissioners had visited that morning.

'Try them, Messieurs. Here are the glasses and twenty-seven casks of my best vintage, from which you will assuredly be able to pick the best. I shall trust your judgement.'

The ambassador accepted this as a well-deserved compliment and took from the servant's hands a hollow tube made of tin, plunged it into the opening of the cask which was against the wall, stopped up the upper end with his large thumb and withdrawing the instrument, poured into his own glass and those of his companions two fingers of white wine drawn from the very centre of the barrel. Then all three together they raised their glasses up to the little window through which the light entered the cellar, and gently, with many tiltings and expert movements, made the rays of light pass through the new liquor and judged what character the light acquired in it. However, I did not learn what their feelings about it were, for, with the same earnestness, they immediately brought the glasses to their lips, ran the mouthful of white wine back and forth between their cheeks, swallowed some, spat out the rest, turning aside out of politeness, and then gave thought and looked at each other. There were frowns, nods, little sighs, but not a single word was uttered. Judgement was not passed until the twenty-seventh witness had been heard.

My old friend went out after saying goodbye to the three, leaving his servant, unusually, to do the honours of the harvest.

'There,' he said, taking a path which led up through the vines, 'these are the delegates appointed by universal suffrage by the members of our "Sociétés" in the villages. They go back centuries, our Sociétés. They are called Le Coq, La Joie, L'Union, Le Laurier. They are very numerous in the whole Loire basin, and probably elsewhere, though I haven't gone into this last point. The pretext for these Sunday get-togethers is the game of boules, when the peasants come especially to chat to each other and to drink wine; they know where it comes from, how much it costs, and they know they can trust it. Yes, Monsieur, our rural Sociétés have remained faithful to their traditions. When townspeople were committing errors of taste, errors that might go down in history, the Sociétés continued to choose the same wines, through the same elected members. They have been the conservators of white wine. They are devoted to it. The commissioners we have just left were appointed a few weeks ago to accomplish today's mission. Charged with choosing the wine to be currently consumed, they must already be making their purchases, and it is the steward of the Société who will put the seven or eight casks into bottles which will refresh the throats of the players of boules. They are allowed to claim expenses for their journeys. On those days if someone comes looking for them at home the woman of the house proclaims with a grand gesture: "They are in the cellars." It is their practice to come to me last and to buy two or three of my best barrels, from among those which will provide the corked, that is to say sealed, wine, and which the richest will sample with respect. Those wines will be put into bottles by the three commissioners themselves, one of whom is a landowning peasant, the other a vet and the third a wine grower. It will happen when the moon is waning, when there is no wind and when you can count seventeen spires from the top of our hillsides.'

As he talked, we were climbing up between the rows of vines which were marvellously straight, and whose newly pruned branches had pearls of sap at each cut.

'My vines are weeping,' said the doctor: 'Spring is under the earth.'

And he raised his cap in a youthful fashion to salute the future wine harvest, when the servant ran up to say:

'Monsieur, I have sold the best three, two at one hundred and eighty and the other at two hundred and ten!'

The Cattle Man

Daniel Boulanger

I was out walking near Senonches. A long trek in wild weather had exhausted me and, as often happens, I was searching for a word stuck down a dark crack of my memory which all my efforts only succeeded in obliterating altogether. Let's see now, I said to myself over and over again, the horse neighs, the frog croaks, the pheasant ... what does the pheasant do? I knew the word, I'd used it all my life, but it was not, as they say so erroneously, on the tip of my tongue. A hot drink would do me good, and I was yearning for a bar. In a quarter of an hour or so I'd be at Senonches, and there ...

A forest warden appeared down a track on a bicycle. I accosted him.

'Excuse me,' I said, 'what is the word for the cry of a pheasant?'

I'd said it with a smile, gently, almost timid. The warden, whose feet hadn't touched the ground but who had gone past, I think, with every intention of stopping, turned round to get a look at me, jerked his head and pushed down hard on the pedals.

Surely, I said to myself, I don't look like a nutter?

The café I was thinking of is just on the way into town: it sits at an angle between the main road and another street. The storm was blowing up rough behind me. The forest creaked. I felt as if I was already amongst its future furniture, in one of those old, cold, high-backed sitting-room suites which groan and crumple and whose creaking skin-and-bone occupants sit and tear at their memories, scratching around, looking for a word ... I reached *Au Bon Coin*. Four men were deep in discussion at the entrance, and I said without thinking twice—

'Excuse me, *messieurs*. Can you help at all? The horse neighs, the elephant trumpets ...'

'The elephant?'

'Yes, but what does a pheasant do?'

'You what?'

I repeated the question, but with less of a smile. One of the men, bleary-eyed, breathed wine all over me.

'The pheasant?'

'Yes, the pheasant.'

He turned back to the others and I saw them glance at each other.

'Never mind,' I said, about to turn back.

A strong hand grabbed my arm, and I found myself surrounded by the four men, in a fug of onion, sweat, and well-manured cloth. I succumbed briefly to the smell: my drunken companions—particularly the one with the black beret pulled down over his tiny close-set eyes—were obviously not in joking mood.

'I don't suppose,' said the youngest, 'I don't suppose . . .'

'Let me through,' I said.

'I don't suppose,' he said, unable to go on.

The old one, whose eyes had now narrowed to become a single eye, poked me with his finger.

'You wouldn't be the Cattle Man, by any chance?'

I heard the click. The youngest had loaded his gun and was holding it at arm's length. 'Tell me,' I asked, now that it had come back to me, *the pheasant squawks, the pheasant squawks* . . .

'Tell me, the horse neighs, the elephant I know, but what about the pheasant?'

'Yesterday,' said the owner, who wore three jumpers flattened by time and sweat in ragged layers over his chest, 'yesterday, up at the crossroads, was that you? With the black van? And the dogs?'

'You must be mistaken. Now then, my round!'

'We don't drink with the Cattle Man.'

'I've never known anyone turn down a drink!' I could feel myself going yellow.

'You haven't answered the question,' said the owner, pouring something from a bottle.

A squeal of tyres made us all swivel towards the door. Policemen were getting out of a car.

'Cheers!'

'Cheers!'

'How much do I owe you?'

'Nothing,' said the owner. 'We'll see you again.'

I nodded to the assembled company and set off for the town centre, where I asked what time the next bus left for Chartres.

'Apparently,' said a traveller sitting on the next bench, 'apparently they've got a lead on that robber.'

'The cattle?'

'Isn't it awful? Apparently he's slaughtered more than a dozen, round and about. They only find the heads.'

'A butcher?'

'Serious muscle, whoever he is.'

I shivered, but the fear and disgust were tinged with a certain pride.

Where Are the Children?

Colette

It was a large house with a high attic room perched on top. The steep gradient of the street meant that the stables and sheds, chicken runs, wash-house, and milk-shed were of necessity packed tightly around a closed courtyard at the bottom.

When I leaned over the garden wall I could scratch the top of the chicken coop with my fingers. The Upper Garden looked down over the Lower Garden, a narrow, sheltered kitchen garden given over to aubergines and peppers, in which the scent of tomato leaves in July blended with the perfume of the ripe apricots on the espaliers. In the Upper Garden were two identical fir trees, a walnut tree in whose unforgiving shade no flower survived, some roses, neglected patches of lawn, a broken arbour... A stout iron fence running alongside the Rue des Vignes at the bottom ought to have afforded the two gardens some protection, but in my time it was permanently bent out of shape, for it had been wrenched from its cement on the wall and forced up in the air by the unyielding arms of a wisteria that had grown there for a hundred years.

The front of the house on the Rue de l'Hospice was a blackened, inelegant façade with a double flight of steps and large windows. It was an old-village, bourgeois house but the steep slope of the street rather undermined its dignified air, and the front steps limped—six on one side and ten on the other.

A large, imposing house, rather forbidding, with its bell like the ones you see on the doors of orphanages, an entrance with a great big bolt like gaols used to have, a house that smiled on nothing but its own garden. The back, which was hidden from passers-by, golden in the sunshine, was cloaked in mixed wisteria and trumpet vines, that grew over a sort of frame made of iron giving way under the weight and that sagged in the middle like a hammock but provided some shade for the small paved terrace and the step up into the living room... Need

I describe the rest, with my inadequate words? I would not manage to make you see what shines so brightly in my memory—the red tendrils of a Virginia creeper brought down by its own weight and still clinging to some branches of pine as it falls. Those huge clumps of lilac with their tight little florets, blue in the shade and crimson in the sun and so quickly withering, as if stifled by their own exuberance, are long dead and will never be resurrected into the light on my account: nor will the terrifying moonlight—silver, lead-grey, mercury, sharp facets of amethyst, the piercing splinters of sapphires—which fell from a particular blue glass pane in the shed at the bottom of the garden.

I know that the house and the garden are still there, but what good is that if the magic has gone from them, if the secret is lost which unlocked a world—the light, the scents, the harmony of the trees and the birds, the murmur of human voices already interrupted by death—I am no longer worthy to inhabit? . . .

It sometimes happened, in the days when a family lived in this house and this garden, that an open book on the paving of the terrace or on the grass, a skipping-rope snaking across a path, or a tiny garden edged with pebbles and planted with flower heads would reveal the presence of children of various ages. But these signs were scarcely ever accompanied by shouts or the laughter of children, and the dwelling place, warm and full of people, bore an odd resemblance to those houses that at the end of the holidays are so abruptly emptied of all their gaiety. The silence, the enclosed wind in the walled garden, the pages of the book thumbed by an invisible sprite—everything seemed to be asking: Where are the children?

That was when my mother, small and round, before the passing years had robbed her body of its flesh, would appear underneath the old iron arch that had been bent to the left by the wisteria. She would gaze at the mass of green leaves, lift up her head and shout out to the skies:

'The children! Where are the children?'

Where were they? Nowhere. Her cry went through the garden, hit the high wall of the hay house and came echoing back feebly, exhausted: 'child-ren'.

Nowhere. My mother threw her head back and gazed up to heaven as if she were expecting a flight of children on wings to descend! After a moment she would shout the same thing again, and then, weary of interrogating the heavens, would break the dried bell off a red-horned poppy with her fingernail, scratch at a rosebush sequinned with greenfly, put the first walnuts into her pocket, shake her head at the thought of the children that had disappeared, and go back into the house. But up above her head, gleaming in among the leaves of the walnut tree, was the tilted, angular face of a child who was stretched out like a tomcat along a large branch, keeping very quiet. Perhaps a less short-sighted mother would have guessed the reason for the rapid bowing of the tops of the two fir trees, a movement that was quite unlike those made by the sudden gusts of October. And in the square window below the pulley for the fodder would she not have noticed, had she screwed up her eyes, those two faint marks in the hay: the face of a young boy and his book? But she had given up every attempt to find us and all hope of reaching us. Our strange turbulence was wholly without noise. I do believe there were never more unruly, and yet never more silent, children. And only now do I find this surprising. Nobody ever required us to be so serenely silent or so unsociable. My 19-year-old brother who constructed hydrotherapy machines out of rolls of cloth, wire, and glass pipes did not prevent my younger brother of 14 from taking a watch to pieces or giving a faultless adaptation on the piano of a tune or a part of a symphony that he had heard in the town; nor even from taking an unfathomable delight in decorating the garden with small tombstones cut out of cardboard, each bearing beneath its cross the name, epitaph, and genealogy of some imaginary deceased... My sister whose hair was too long could read interminably without a break. The two boys would brush past and seemed not even to notice the little girl, enchanted, absent, and she was not disturbed. When I was small I had all the time in the world to run along after the boys as they went striding off into the woods in pursuit of the Poplar Admiral, the Purple Emperor, or the Scarce Swallowtail, or hunting grass-snakes or collecting the tall foxgloves in July deep in the woods spattered with red pools of heather... But I followed them in silence, gathering blackberries, wild cherries, or flowers; I beat down the undergrowth and crossed the waterlogged fields like a little dog going its own way with no need to explain himself to anyone...

'Where are the children?' She would appear suddenly, out of breath, in her constant quest, like an overprotective mother-dog with her head up, sniffing the breeze. Her arms wrapped in white cloth were a sign that she had just been kneading the biscuit dough or making a pudding with its red-hot sauce of rum and preserves. If she was wrapped in a capacious blue apron then she had been washing the havanese dog and sometimes she would be waving a strip of crackly yellow paper, the paper from the butcher's. That was because she was hoping to gather together, at the same time as her scattered children, her vagabond cats, hungry for raw meat.

With the traditional shout came, with the same urgent entreaty, a reminder of what time it was:

'Four o'clock! They haven't come in for tea! Where are the children?...Half past six! Are they coming in for supper? Where are the children?'...

What a lovely voice she had and how I should weep now with delight to hear it...Our only sin, our one misdeed, was our silence, and a kind of miraculous vanishing. For our innocent purposes, for a freedom that was never refused us, we would jump over the iron fence, leaving our shoes behind, using an unnecessary ladder for the way back, the low wall that belonged to a neighbour. Our worried mother, with her subtle sense of smell, would be able to detect on us the wild garlic from a distant gully or the mint from the grass-covered marshes. The damp pocket of one of the boys hid the trunks that he had taken with him to the feverous ponds while the youngest, with her knees ripped to pieces and her scraped elbow, was bleeding quietly under plasters made out of spiders' webs and milled pepper bound with ribbons of grass...

'Tomorrow I shall lock you up! The whole lot of you, do you hear, the whole lot!'

Tomorrow...Tomorrow the oldest, sliding along the slate roof where he was installing a water-tank, would break his collar-bone and lie silently, politely, half-unconscious at the foot of the wall waiting for someone to come and pick him up. Tomorrow the younger son would get a six-metre ladder full in his forehead, and not say a word but come back meekly, with an egg-shaped purple lump between his eyes...

'Where are the children?'

Two are at rest. The others are growing older, day by day. If there is a place where people wait for us when we die, the woman who waited for us is still worrying about the two still alive remaining on earth. For the eldest of all she will at least no longer be gazing at the black window pane in the evenings:

'Oh I can feel that child is not happy...Oh I can tell she is in pain...'

For the elder of the two boys her heart no longer misses a beat in the darkness as she hears the wheels of a doctor's cab in the snow, or the clip-clopping of the grey mare. But I know that for the two who remain she is wandering and searching still, invisible and tormented that she is not looking after them as she ought:

'Where are they, where are the children?...'

The Vanishing

Louis Pergaud

'Burgundy was a happy place in those days'... and so, too, was the Franche-Comté. Every autumn, vats full of beautiful wine the colour of onion skins gushed forth from the bunches of poulsard and were brought down from the slopes of Arbois, Poligny, and Salins; and the ruddy-faced wine-growers gave thanks to the Lord, whose sun had put life into the burgeoning shoots and filled their barrels.

At that time, and let us not fix it more precisely, there lived two good friends, of the kind you hardly ever come across nowadays, one in Salins, and the other high up on the plateau of Cornabeuf, two old companions who had been united from early childhood by the bonds of brotherly feeling and also by their many conversations about Art in this little provincial backwater; a relationship as good-humoured as it was passionate, their conversations enlivened by the red September cordial that so cheers the heart and quenches the thirst.

And so the poet Étienne Lecourt, an admirer of Casimir Delavigne, and the author—not honoured in his own country, for none is prophet there—the author, as we were saying, of *The Echoes of the Heart*, held in high and particular esteem a musician by the name of Jacques Mirondeau, who was older than him and whose happiness lay in composing tunes on his violin. Like his friend Étienne he had lived without anyone telling him what to do until the age of 45, when he had married, for the love of music, a Mademoiselle Euphrasie Jeannerot, who was twenty years older than him; she was fervently devoted to harmony, and spent all the hours she did not dedicate to her housework at her piano.

Marriage did in no wise diminish the affection these two men had for one another. On the contrary, when the musician, for some reason, left it longer than usual before going down to the town, the poet would often go up and pay a friendly and courteous visit to the mountain dweller and his wife.

That very day Étienne Lecourt had climbed up to Cornabeuf by the steep, rocky path, which wound its precipitous way up the mountain, and all three had passed a delightful afternoon—Jacques, bow in hand, and Madame Mirondeau at the piano—making music and discussing the latest romantic literary efforts, in particular those of *Mocieu* Victor Hugo, who was, according to Étienne, a disgrace to French literature and the laughing stock of Europe.

Towards evening the poet took his umbrella, gallantly kissed Madame Mirondeau's hand, and said goodbye.

'I'll come with you a little way,' declared Jacques, changing the slippers embroidered by his wife for a pair of clogs. 'I'll bring back the milk with me.'

The two friends left, went into one or two houses, and then continued their discussion, which apparently had not been been exhausted, because, still deep in conversation, they walked along in the failing twilight, the one carrying his jug and the other his umbrella...

For three days people living in the little town of Salins, the commune of Cornabeuf, and all the villages round about had been puzzled and worried; relatives, friends, and neighbours were anxious because three full days had gone by and there was absolutely no news of the poet and the musician.

Was this double disappearance the result of some terrible accident or violent crime?

Half an hour after her husband had left, Madame Mirondeau had begun to be a little uneasy at his prolonged absence; she went out to look for him, but could not see him coming and, so, throwing a scarf round her shoulders, she set off anxiously to find out what had happened.

First she went to Gaulenot the innkeeper and he told her that the two men had had one drink at his bar and then left again, still discussing poetic metre or the metric system, he wasn't sure which, because he was not learned like those gentlemen.

The man in the cheese shop, when questioned, informed her that Jacques, accompanied by the gentleman with the long hair, had left with his milk as usual. That was all he knew.

So where had he gone after that? In the clothes he was wearing, he certainly would not have dreamed of going down into the town.

Madame Mirondeau returned home, having managed to make her neighbours share her concern, and persuaded them to set off in search of her husband without delay; which was not hard to do, for they were all very fond of him.

Half a dozen of them, carrying lanterns, started out on the path to Salins that the two men must have taken. Up as far as the top of the hill they saw nothing, but at the foot of the wooden cross, erected at the place where the path begins to climb the mountain, they found the musician's milk jug, still full and with its layer of cream on top— proof positive that he had passed that way.

After putting their heads together and giving the matter their consideration, they concluded that their neighbour must have accompanied his friend down to Salins, and that he would probably come up again in the course of the evening. Nevertheless, to set their minds at rest and just in case there had been an accident of some kind, they went almost halfway down the path, shouting out Jacques' name in every direction. All that came back to them in the quiet, starlit night were the faithful echoes from the valley as their cries were repeated mockingly in the distance.

Madame Mirondeau had gone to bed, somewhat reassured. But the next day when Jacques had still not returned, one of the neighbours, who had some shopping to do in the market, set off at first light to go and find out what he could.

The man from Cornabeuf, arriving at the poet Étienne Lecourt's house, on the side of the vineyards at Belin, found the door open and the place deserted. He called: there was no answering voice. He went upstairs and found nobody.

Greatly puzzled and worried, he went down into the streets of the town and as he went about his business, told the people he met about the strange and mysterious disappearance.

No one had seen the poet or musician the night before, and very soon the whole town knew about it. As it was market day, rumours spread amongst the country folk, increasing rapidly throughout the canton, like the circles of a stone in a pond; and as soon as their friend came back and the authorities had been hurriedly informed, the good people of Cornabeuf lost no time in setting off in every direction to scour the mountainside.

They explored every nook and cranny in the rocks. Some brave people went down unexplored precipices, using ropes knotted end to end. They examined the most isolated and wildest places. They searched the hollows of the river. They visited the sleaziest bars in town and houses of even worse repute. But there was no sign of either of the men who had vanished.

That had been going on for three days, and anxiety was mounting with the fatigue and the enervation of searching in vain.

What could have happened? Jacques Mirondeau and Étienne Lecourt must certainly be dead. But where were their decaying bodies? Had some foreign prowler, some unknown assassin, murdered them on the mountain and, stripping them of their possessions, carried off their corpses and buried them somewhere else?

The puzzle seemed insoluble. The people of Cornabeuf, feeling the horror of this mystery weighing upon them, barricaded themselves into their houses in the evenings, while in Salins the sages of the town talked about the old traditions and the bad old days and said they should set up patrols each evening to keep watch over the sleeping town.

As dawn was breaking on the fourth day and, gathered together in impressive numbers, they were discussing the latest possibilities, suddenly a small boy pointed out that there seemed to be smoke coming from the poet's house.

His father, telling him he was a little fool and giving him a box on the ears for joining in adults' conversation without being asked, was nevertheless forced to acknowledge, along with the others round him, that the boy had a point. And, much intrigued, all present hurried off in the direction of the house of Étienne Lecourt.

They went in, just as the farmer from Cornabeuf had done, and on going through the whole of the ground floor, found absolutely nothing. Undaunted, they went up to the floor above and explored that as well. But neither there nor in the attic could they discover where the smoke was coming from.

However, as logically, and even proverbially, there can be no smoke without fire, they did not give up, and one behind the other they descended the staircase that led to the basement.

Just as in most of the houses built into the hillside, the basement is only half a basement, that is to say, half of it is underground and the other part is open. In front of the cellar there was a sort of storeroom. They went in.

At a table, laden with a hunk of bread, half a Gruyère cheese, and an inumerable quantity of empty bottles, the two friends they thought were dead were talking away to each other like philosophers. On the stove, which had just been lit, a piece of meat was turning into a cinder.

Having reached the cross on top of the Côte, at the point when their discussion was at its most intense, Étienne Lecourt had persuaded his old friend to go as far as Salins with him, inviting him to share, in a brotherly way, his bread, cheese, and a piece of veal he intended to roast.

Jacques Mirondeau had willingly agreed and for the last three days they had been there discussing literature and music, first one and then the other, with their cheese and their bottles of wine on the table in front of them. The farmer from Cornabeuf had not seen a thing and no more had the people of Salins, for all were ignorant of the fact that the poet Lecourt, so as to be nearer his wine-cellar, had thought it a good idea to transform his basement into a kitchen and dining room.

Moreover, the arrival of their friends and neighbours did not seem to impinge on the high-minded concerns of the two artists, and the good people of Salins, aghast, heard the poet Étienne Lecourt tersely conclude their solemn and courteous debate with the words:

'Yes indeed, my dear Jacques, as I have just had the honour of explaining to you, and you have understood me completely: at bottom our *Mocieu* Victor Hugo is a good-for-nothing.'

Julie

Jacques Chardonne

In December 1945 I returned to Mâchecoul to clear out
some things, say hail and farewell to Clothilde's empty
house and my goodbyes to Patrice and Julie. They now
spent the whole year at La Nocle, their former country
retreat near Mâchecoul.

I had delayed my visit to La Nocle until my last day.
The servant told me that Patrice had not been there for
four months. I was not surprised. At that time, a lot of
people were on the move, and some very moral people in
that region had been shocked by Patrice's conduct.

I asked to see Julie and waited for her in the drawing-
room. The room was well polished and bitterly cold. The
very cold felt antique and seemed to emanate from the

depths of the draperies. This house, a former factory producing cannonballs, first became a hotel and then was rented by Patrice and Julie, who used it as their summer residence. They had the roof altered and piled the furniture belonging to two families up in the bedrooms, which had been gradually abandoned by the children. Trees, dating from the time when the factory had been there, grew profusely in the damp soil, and veiled the neighbouring marshes. At this time of the year the Virginia creeper was spreading its dark mesh over the façade, and beyond it you could see the roof of the farm and the walls of the vegetable garden.

I couldn't hear a sound. I was used to waiting like this in the drawing-room, whenever I visited La Nocle. Although Julie had lived in Paris since her wedding, she had never lost her provincial habits. You almost never see women out and about in small towns. They stay shut up in their rooms. The rest of the house belongs to the men and the streets belong to the devil. As time passed, this inclination of Julie's for shutting herself away grew ever more pronounced. In Paris she was quite invisible.

When she sent for me to come up and I went into her room, she was enveloped in a grey shawl, sitting beside a tiled stove. She extracted one hand from under her woollen garments, held it out to me and put it back again on the warm rim of the stove. The childish hand, very white and extremely delicate, with its huge pearl engagement ring, and the innocent brilliance of her bright eyes, were all that was left of the young girl she had once been. In her place a sort of grey cloud had taken the form of a vague, sweet, matronly woman, who was a stranger to me and who seemed rather unreal.

She said:

'Patrice is in Charente.'

'For long?'

'For a very long time, I believe.'

'I'll see him then. I'm going to Charente too.'

'I promised not to give anyone his address.'

'Well he's definitely not in Royan.'

And I repeated the word: 'Royan . . .'

This name had a special resonance for us. It was the town where we spent our holidays when we were children. Royan, with its girls, Royan with its dazzling sun in the middle of the day. Julie had been one of those girls. Patrice was a boy of 20 from Paris who stayed in the Villa Grisélidis. I joined them as soon as I could from Limoges. Every summer for five years there was a little group of us. Patrice picked out Julie. She was 14, I think, when he said to me: 'Have you noticed Julie? She's going to be very nice-looking.' For five years she went out with him, subjected to the will of this man who fascinated her with his impatient desires.

When I saw Julie again at different times in her life, and now looking so pale and oppressed, I always thought of that aching passion from those summers of our youth when the most fervent love had lodged in her heart and head. She remained now as if suspended above the earth, somewhat distracted, breathless, suffering from the loss of warmth in her life, hankering after a lost love which was right beside her but which she no longer recognized.

'How are you?'

'I can't sleep. It's my heart.'

'You like life in the country.'

'I don't go out. I can't walk.'

'Lucky you have good servants. Now La Nocle is yours.'

'Patrice bought La Nocle for me last year and then left.'

'He had to.'

'He believes he had to.'

'Have you any news of the children?'

'They are fine.'

I asked some more questions but her answers were short. I was her oldest friend and I knew her well. I treated her a little as though she were mistress of a castle ruined by the cost of its upkeep. She dared not say anything in front of me. No doubt she thought I was watching her too closely while I spoke.

There was a fair in Jarnac the day I arrived. Men had come from the surrounding districts in their caps and their black hats. There were no animals or carts to be seen, but in the cafés consultations took place during which invisible beasts changed hands. Everything became symbolic.

I still wasn't sure whether I'd stay with my daughter or rent a room... For a time that provided me with an aim when I was out cycling. I would look for a place in the country to live. It's good when we can attach to natural things some idea that they might be useful or beautiful; without it, they might not hold our attention for very long.

After many bicycle rides I got to hear of a neglected lodge situated down at the bottom of a field by the river; its name was Corbigny, in memory of the viscount who used to live there. This slate-covered building in dark stone, decorated with a light iron balcony, had been built by a royal employee and was not local in style.

There I found Patrice in a high-ceilinged room whose silken wallpaper had seen better days.

'Yes, here I am. Have a seat, since you've tracked me down. I'm sorry there aren't many. I left Mâchecoul because I wasn't happy there, though people weren't being unkind to me. Really, I went away out of courtesy. I am surprised I wasn't shot. They persecute puerile reactionaries full of fine sentiments, and let me go. Can't they see I'm a heretic, a gallows-bird? So I have condemned myself to be a perpetual recluse in this crumbling lodge where I shall end my days without even bothering to have it repaired. I have broken with all my usual habits, even the senseless one of pondering the future and the human race. Before I worry about humanity I'd like to know what is simmering in the entrails of the earth and liberates itself in the volcanic puffs we have just had examples of. Some day it will all be explained. It will be made very clear. But it's none of my business. In fact, I believe nothing in this world is any concern of mine. I couldn't care less about the paltry everyday events; they are almost always unreal and change everything and nothing. What does an event matter when you don't know what happens afterwards? I often hear it said that people have got things wrong, but I never know exactly who they mean by that. Superficial men like me and superficial nations can cope with events very well. They don't give a damn about them. Serious people believe in events. They are shaped by accidents, which are the mechanics of the atmosphere. I don't want to see anyone apart from my charming Angèle, that dotty old girl who let you in. She's always cheery. I don't ask any more of my neighbour... Only solitude perhaps still holds some interest for me. It intrigues me, like those oriental temples which are forbidden to the profane.

Solitude is, I believe, propitious to the revelations of the spirit. Family, streets, work impede the spirit . . . Will I have total solitude? I see a few people on the road; but I am shielded from pernicious distractions. Yet in monasteries monks are kept busy with mechanical occupations. Perhaps too deep a reflectiveness is not favourable to visitations of the spirit. What frightens me about the world which is coming into being is the loss of our little earthly pleasures. Everything which has been pleasurable or of any concern to men will come to an end. Society is becoming insipid. In the old days our fathers went to their clubs and kept expensive mistresses. Simply somewhere to go. Nowadays you stay at home. It's a dreadful thing, a home with children, a loving wife, devoted, sensitive, demanding, and whom you always cause to suffer, because you are a man. And leisure is terrible . . . Of course madmen have things to amuse them. But I never played games, even as a child. I had serious pursuits even then. Later on, I never played cards or did gardening or took up philosophy. I only had one leisure pursuit in my life: my business. Julie thought I was a lover of women. But women never troubled me. Julie was enough claim on my heart. A long-standing relationship like ours is not a very common thing in Paris. When you have what is honourable and excellent as your guiding principle, the profits are small. But I liked the warm atmosphere of my workplace. That warmth came from the involvement of the staff in the dignity of the business. It was a thing we shared. How we looked after it! And what confidence that it would last! Strange, isn't it? The faith of us unbelievers, knowing that all that work, so poorly rewarded, and all that business, seeming so solid, would disappear before we did, or soon enough after, like every human thing. That maniacal luxuriating in the work was what gave us pleasure . . . I have left everything to the children. A father's death is a long time coming. I have anticipated it. A father's love is a beautiful thing, sometimes . . . Love in the abstract . . . Not a stifling love . . . At present I want silence. I know words have no sense, not in politics or philosophy or in love.'

'I saw Julie . . .'

This man who was demanding silence would not stop talking. He was in fact talking so as not to say anything, to belie his loneliness, interrupting me, and, in his paradoxical anger, hiding from himself what he did not want to know.

'I saw Julie . . .'

'She is fine, I know. She is happy at La Nocle. She wanted to live in the country. Now the children are married, things couldn't be better for her. She loves flowers so much!'

'She isn't happy and she's worried about the future. She is not weeping. She cannot weep when you are absent from her, but I think it is bad for her.'

'She has always worried about the future, always sure she will lose everything. She is always looking for something. She loses things on purpose. In the thing she has mislaid she seeks whatever she believes is lost or has abandoned her: absent children, the husband who is never enough of a husband... These gentle women who live by their fine feelings have a unique ability to torment themselves, which is hard for the other person to bear. They are very inventive in the ways of tyranny. Now Julie has trouble with her heart. She refuses to see a doctor or take any remedy. When I ask Courdaveau to come, she locks the door. Courdaveau says it's nothing, the suffocating sensations she has are only nerves. I am not sure. I am careful what I say. A word out of place could kill her. When you get to my age you are no longer in control of yourself, you get irascible, even coarse, perhaps you say things you shouldn't. I'm afraid of hurting her... These souls whose vocation is love always strain after the dreams of their youth... Julie is still 20... She's a child... She has a child's eyes, tears, moods, she is someone whom life has passed over without extinguishing the flame. As she gets older and progressively more innocent the features of childhood become more pronounced in her. Of course she has been several different women: a devoted mother, a detached mother; she has loved to travel, and she has had a passion for the life of a recluse, she was thin, now she is well-covered, but through all these metamorphoses there remains the indelible basis of the emotions. What strange vitality the heart possesses! In my office I had some respite, but that continual tête-à-tête creates an atmosphere in which I can't breathe. I had good reasons for leaving and Julie understood them. The truth is that I wish to live alone. Before I die I shall reach a part of myself which I sense, yet cannot define, and which solitude will reveal to me. In families you give in to a diabolical temptation: the wish to criticize your nearest and dearest. Even if you become the fount of wisdom as you grow older, that's the stumbling block: intolerance. There is no question of divorce between us, nor even of a legal separation. Marriage is a bond one cannot break without denying what one is oneself. But in the end each partner speaks a language that is unintelligible to the other... Julie will not change. She was badly educated. I suppose no education is possible in matters of the heart. Is it love or is it one's character which is responsible for this desire for possession, for absolute love, which ruins everything?... I have found that women who are so demanding in matters of love and who do not accept human mediocrity are all the same in the way they conduct themselves. They have grand ideas. They are destined for heaven but have lost their way. The truth is, they are great ladies.'

'You educated Julie.'

'I had forgotten that. But I am not the boy of 20 I once was. That's the difference...At La Nocle she has fuel, she can keep warm. She has everything she needs.'

'She looked very pale sitting beside her stove.'

'I was no good to her. She will be better off without me, you'll see. Gradually she will gain the kind of contentment that widows acquire...I am glad to say. I could not bear to think that she was suffering.'

'Have you any books?'

'It's time I read Grégoire de Tours. I haven't got a comfortable armchair. I have got rid of the radio. I'd had enough of love songs. Apart from the frightening mingling of two lives that marriage entails, that carries on consuming you till the very end have *you* got any happy memories of love? Come now! They are always shameful. You must have dinner with me. I have nothing to offer you but we will pretend to eat. Angèle will put plates on the table and it will look as though we are having a meal. You can't get anything in this region, there's even less than last year. But we can't complain. Royan was destroyed for reasons of protocol with fifteen hundred killed. People hardly talk about it any more. Events that affect people for real matter to them less than their perception of the situation. All that is now part and parcel of the idea of a great benefaction and a new hope. We have seen blessed martyrs.

But more often the ungrateful wretches to whom Dante promises a place in his Inferno because they wept when they should have rejoiced. Julie has had everything she longed for, without ever recognizing the fact. She has always complained because she had some idea of having missed out, and she never took any pleasure in anything except in this gloomy illusion. I am a communist. Communists bring with them the confidence in a better life, and forbid all doubt and despair. They are psychologists! Whatever you do with society, if you leave people to their own devices, they will only complain about it ... Do you remember the Charentais society of the old days? What peace there was! People didn't know what to do with those good times and some were already beginning to bang their drums. The people of the Charente are quite capable of overthrowing a regime that has suited them and served them well. They have learned their demands by heart and get tangled up in their complaints. In France revolutions are brought about by prejudice, always through a misunderstanding. This is likely to happen when men lose their sense of the connectedness between things, and that sense has greatly diminished among the French. They are surprised by everything, even by what they have desired. I have never been able to make Julie understand this relationship between things, this connection between cause and effect.'

I made a move to retrieve my coat that was draped over the back of a chair against the stove, and he said with an anxious look:

'There's no hurry. It's still broad daylight. Won't you really have dinner with me?'

He spoke faster and faster in order to keep me there. He spoke about man's inability to bear leisure, about work which had no meaning, about the Church, about the history of religions, about the end of the world. And Julie's name came up constantly in this maelstrom of ideas. He talked about women, whom he regarded as despotic creatures, relentless towards men, possessed by insane jealousy, like ferrets by nature and with the eyes of a lynx. Then he spoke of the sanctity of marriage and immediately declared, like the good Cathar that he was, that marriage is properly speaking a sinful state because it causes evil thoughts. He had a horror of the human species, without making any distinction between its component parts.

'As for private attachments, I know what they are like. They rapidly degenerate into tangles and complexities, the divorce of the people involved, insane egotism and hallucinations. Foolish the person who places his trust in man! Do you know that saying? It is in the *Imitation*. There's something of the Christian and the stoic in all of us. That is what we have in common. A small thing, not amounting to much.'

He had abandoned his business, his passion, his goal, his principles, the pleasures of life in order to go beyond what he possessed. Once emerged from the shell that he had so carefully created around him, I found him very denuded. Lacking any definite faith, I had nothing to offer him. Perhaps I hoped for some obsessive illness that would occupy his mind. In this sparsely furnished room with its high windows, he seemed out on a promontory offering himself up to some light that he was unable to reach and finding only boredom in this emptiness, hurt by the wounds of a man turning against himself. This image of a promontory came into my mind because I was looking through a dusty window at the water in the river which was covering the fields, a frozen expanse of pewter gleaming before my eyes, with half-submerged trunks of trees, a black scribble of branches on the inert and pallid land.

I had left Patrice abruptly. The man was too full of himself to bother with the vague niceties of hello and goodbye.

Halfway up a hill I got off my bicycle. In the fields overlooking the floods it was another season. A man was pruning his vines, and the sound of his secateurs reminded me of the alarm cry of the warbler. Oaks and pines were covering part of the hill. I saw what looked like a great fire in the setting sun. Against a background of burnished copper could be seen the slender jumble of branches in fine arabesques of Indian ink. In the warmer air, in the brighter sky, were the first stirrings of spring, already signalled by the faint call of a bird. As I walked along the edge of the oakwood I stopped to look at the crisp carpet of ferns and the leaves, now paling somewhat by the end of the winter, and I tried to determine the exact nuance of its tones of pinkish ochre.

Jarnac is a small town the colour of pearl, where all life has taken refuge inside the houses. No noise, scarcely any people in the streets, only pretty façades of dressed stone which look as if they are made from old ivory or old silver, high windows with grey shutters. A town of shade and light and blessed peace.

I was hoping to live there in a room I had rented. After ten years of idleness, the time had come to write a novel with Patrice as subject. He had characteristics not unlike mine; others which were foreign to me, so in one person suggesting both the self and the non-self.

Before shutting myself away in this fearsome room, I looked for a table big enough to spread out my papers.

I am no good at what is called meditation and I have never really understood the work of a writer. Above all he must be wary of his own ideas. His thinking is never mature enough. His inspiration is full of pitfalls. Moreover in France an author does himself a disservice when he writes. He will be blamed both for his faults and for his qualities.

Boredom threatened and I was about to set to work out of despair, when Charlie Alcot's aeroplane touched down on Cognac aerodrome. I had known Charlie in Boston in 1936. We had much to say about the world and I hurried over to Cognac to see him. Our first conversation was short. He held the same opinions as me about people and events. I find it easy to agree with foreigners. It is between French people that conversation is difficult. They don't speak the same language and each knows only his own dialect.

Charlie offered to take me to Morocco. Here was an opportunity to escape my work. What a chance! But chance frightens me. I have never bought a ticket for the lottery, for fear of winning the jackpot. And I dislike promised paradises, it's the old problem of the ill-favoured man who realizes that he must earn every penny by the sweat of his brow. But Charlie carried me off despite myself.

In Africa I received a letter from Julie who had been trying to get hold of me in various places. The old date on the letter made the urgent tone of it all the more pathetic. Julie wanted to see me immediately.

Later, passing through Bordeaux, I had a second letter from Julie. It was the same urgent appeal, reproducing word for word what she had said in her first. I thought she might wait a few days. But then I changed my plans in order to go to La Nocle before I returned to Charente.

Julie received me in her room and looked at me bleakly without comprehending what I was telling her. I mentioned her letters, making it clear that I had come from Bordeaux at her request. She said:

'I am very ill.'

I noticed her lifeless hands, her pale, slightly violet lips, and a certain dullness in her entire being which was sustained by only the faintest of breaths.

'You must look after yourself. Go and see a doctor. You have something wrong with your heart. It can be cured.'

Suddenly a graceful radiance, almost a smile, appeared in her faded eyes. She was speaking, she was listening:

'Do you see Patrice sometimes?'

'I left Charente a long time ago. I've been in Africa and I've come straight here from Bordeaux, but I'm going back to Jarnac and I shall see Patrice then.'

'Do something for me. I have something important to tell him and he must be told of it either after my death or before, whichever you like. As far as he is concerned I am already dead and he will not come back. He will certainly have told you the reasons why he left. Everything he told you was a lie, I am convinced of that. I believe I know the real reason and it is on that subject that I wish to explain myself. You must speak to him tactfully. I will tell you everything in a letter.'

'Tell me now.'

'It would tire me and there are too many details to take in. Take care with the details, they need careful management. You will be able to choose the right moment, soften the blow... That's why I need you. I had thought of writing to Patrice, but a letter is always too short and too cruel. I can write to you. You know when to elaborate or draw a veil over things...'

One sunny, showery day, between winter and spring, when the bushes beside the road still wear their dark winter coat and the blue flame of the distant hills is set in silver, I went to Corbigny. The chain of my bicycle had come off and I made the most of my stop to rehearse my speech. The main thing was the preamble. If you prepare your speech carefully you can say what you please. I had Julie's letter in my pocket, but I knew it by heart anyway. I had foreseen Patrice's interruptions, I had my answers ready, and the whole dialogue was running smoothly through my mind.

From the hall, into which a broad stone staircase cascaded down, I called up to announce my arrival. Patrice was sleeping. I realized that he had got used to a solitary existence. He had made up his mind to sleep. The room he inhabited in his waking hours wore a more human aspect. There was a table, an armchair, and on the table were two files stuffed with papers.

Patrice welcomed me warmly, but without showing any surprise, as though he had seen me only the day before. He seemed unaware that a year had gone by since my last visit. I might have thought it was his fine sensibility that made him refrain from asking banal questions or use common modes of expression, but I rather think it was that people who were not there did not exist for him and that he could not be bothered to hide it.

'I have been to see Julie...'

'I know. She wrote me a lovely letter about you coming to La Nocle. She writes beautiful letters. I've been collecting them since I left. In the old days I didn't notice her letters, I didn't realize how charming they were. You live with a woman for forty years and there's a woman in her, perhaps more than one, who is a stranger to you. Julie is intelligent and sensitive. She has nobility and a kind of innocence which comes from a rare purity of the soul. But I never suspected she could write. When she writes, it is as if things are recreated by her in a soft dawn light. Her letters are very simple...'

He pulled out a paper from one of the files lying on the table.

'This passage, for example: "I do not think it necessary to have Étienne light the fire. In the morning I do not find these duties onerous. They impose on me a discipline that is good for me and lighting the fire is a good way to begin the day. I like to see the flames leap up just as I like to cross the little wood and the garden to fetch the milk, even in cold weather. All my joy derives from nature or from humble things. Human beings are too harsh for me." It's nothing really—but moving, don't you think? If the letter interests you, you can read it. Or this one which is older... It's a different time of the year.'

He reread the letters, and then passed them to me.

'Yes, they are lovely letters and most surprising for anyone coming from La Nocle. I wonder from what depths, in her poor petrified being, Julie can draw such freshness. You would not recognize her, she is scarcely alive... She has asked me to do something for her, it's about something that happened a long time ago which I believe you have not forgotten and which I want to talk to you about... Do you remember a boy called Paul?'

'Paul?... No... Paul who?'

'A boy who used to go to your place about fifteen years ago...'

'Oh, Paul Cabaret. Yes. The son of one of our foremen. He used to come round, I don't know why. He was a boy...'

'Does that name mean anything to you?'

'No. Why? Has he got into trouble?'

'Paul Cabaret doesn't bring to mind anything connected with Julie? Well then...you don't know...'

'What?'

'You have nothing to reproach Julie for?'

'We talked about that last year...I blame her for everything...Perhaps it's my fault...No I don't reproach her for anything in particular.'

'You didn't know that the boy...For some years...You didn't know that Julie had a lover?'

'Julie!'

'She wants me to tell you that if she chose that boy, the most insignificant of the people around you, and the last who might be expected to inspire feelings of love, it was on purpose, because he did not mean anything to her. She knew that she was annoying you, that her love for you was getting on your nerves, and she thought that if she could get interested in another man, she would become more reasonable and you would be happier.'

Patrice said nothing, but he looked towards the window with eyes which seemed to darken; his expression was dreadfully tense and staring. Silence transformed this man who was ordinarily burning with words. The revelation had struck him like a stone. If he had said something, I could have come to his aid. I was armed with explanations and ways to soften the blow. Wounded, he eluded me by his deathly silence.

I had learned my lesson by heart, and had recited it blindly, mechanically, even mindlessly, while Patrice knew nothing. I had resurrected an event which was dormant in darkness, unknown, eradicated, and had made a weapon of it to fling at him. I had been a stupid messenger of fate, the unconscious instrument of the gods who raise and destroy empires, turn justice upside down, and disperse blessings and sufferings randomly for the world to mock at.

I went back home filled with shame. I was an assassin. I dreaded the arrival of the postman, that other bearer of tidings, rather more than usual.

I waited a few weeks, then returned to Corbigny. I saw Angèle perched on a window-sill rubbing away at a window in the full sunshine, as though she were playing a game with the rays of sunshine. The house looked unusually clean. Angèle was able to tell me nothing about

Patrice, who had left without a word the day after my last visit. But she assured me that all was well, because she felt very happy. The impression I got was only of good auspices about the world in general.

I got rid of my bicycle and bought a car that had been scorned by the Germans and rejected by our soldiers, and left for Paris, happy to be travelling in comfort again, and made a detour through Anjou. I remembered a place where the rivers met, where I had once experienced the most beautiful spring. The Sarthe, the Mayenne, the Maine, the Loir, and the Loire all mingle there. You can get lost among rivers and floods. There are bluish waters on the fields, hedges lit with honeysuckle and foxgloves, apple trees with their old branches still entwined, just coming into flower.

But, as I drove along, another thought crossed my mind. These machines that respond so promptly to one's impulses are formidable servants. I was already, without thinking about it, on my way to La Nocle.

As I pulled up under the oak trees I saw Patrice in front of the house. He was overseeing two old men who had become his rather doddery gardeners and who, with their faded old clothes, seemed themselves to be made out of clay.

'It's a bit late for planting,' Patrice said to me, 'but I want Julie to have a bed of roses in front of her window.'

Abruptly he went inside. I watched one of the gardeners carefully wheeling a barrow of earth. Patrice came out again.

'I shan't ask you up. But Julie knows who you are and is pleased. I scarcely leave her side. I think she can breathe more easily if I am nearby. I watch her all night. I don't sleep any more. You can live without sleep. I want her to be happy during her last days. When she says: "My dear Patrice" it is enough. It seems to me then that I have made a success of my life.'

Four Walls

Claude Michelet

Three months ago, Olivier and Christine Laborde, with a combined age of 65, on the strength of the financial loan they had arranged, had crossed the divide that separates the tenant from the home-owner. Their minds were made up; their second child would take his first steps in his own garden, one that belonged to them.

But even though the baby was not expected for another six months, it was time to buy a plot and build the house they had been dreaming of ever since they got married six years ago. For the last two years they had been thinking that their high-rise flat in their home town was too small. It was true that their four-year-old son Julien took up more and more room. As for his mother, she was wanting an extra room to put the new baby in, a bigger kitchen, and a living-room where you wouldn't feel you were suffocating if six people were in it all at the same time. Besides, the more Olivier was involved with his job, the more he was wanting a room of his own to work in peace.

So, determined to go about the matter with the same degree of seriousness and energy that he put into managing his job as a rep in machine tools, he had started to search for the ideal spot. He had found it on a very nice estate that had recently been built, with a pleasant aspect, some two kilometres from Brive-la-Gaillarde.

But when they talked to Maître Jean-François Marsac and told him about the house they had chosen, Olivier and Christine had immediately sensed the lack of enthusiasm on the part of the lawyer; never until now had Monsieur Marsac been so unequivocal in his views.

'You must do as you wish, you are the ones who are buying it,' he said in that measured tone of voice that always inspired sympathy in the people he talked to. 'But yes, since you have asked me what I think, I believe you are making a mistake in choosing this place.' His index finger was on the survey open on his desk.

'But the plot is in a good position,' said Olivier, looking at his wife for approval.

'Yes, we like it a lot,' the young woman agreed.

'And two thousand five hundred square metres is plenty, especially when you have to keep the grass down!' joked Olivier. 'So, do you mind telling us what you think is wrong with this plot?'

'Everything! All right, I'll be frank. You want to build. Fine, but as I've always told my children, building a house is a big undertaking. Oh I know, I am not questioning your wish to own a house. But since I am at least old enough to be your father, that gives me the right to ask: You want to build? All right, but *what* do you want to build?'

'A house, of course.' Olivier was already rather irritated at the way the interview was going.

'Well of course you want to build a house! But what kind? No, don't say anything, I know what you are going to say. You have told me what your financial situation is and you are in a hurry to have a roof over your heads. I conclude that unless you win the lottery, your house will be the usual bottom-of-the-range kind of thing, without any character, that you could move into straight away; a sort of computerized hut drawn out by so-called architects, who all think they are Le Vau or Mansart, but who would not in a million years live in the thing they are proposing to sell you! In short, you are proposing to buy a shoebox, which, thirty years from now, when you will scarcely have finished paying off your loans, will be a complete wreck! That's why they are built like that.'

'I don't understand you,' interjected Olivier, who was getting more and more upset. 'After all, what we want to build is our business and only ours.'

'Of course. But you asked me my opinion and I am giving it.'

'Do you not like modern houses?' Christine enquired.

'No, Madame. Very few of them have any soul.'

'Soul?' insisted the young woman.

'Yes, a life, a past, if you prefer. The sort of charm that gives you the feeling that the house is unique and that it is good to live in and bring up your family in. And even, why not, end your days in, knowing that your children and your grandchildren will inhabit it in their turn and that the four walls will carry on reminding them of you. So they have nothing in common with the terrible housing projects currently disfiguring our countryside!'

'Anyone would think you had something better to offer us!' Olivier remarked with a touch of defiance in his voice.

'Indeed, I do,' said the lawyer, opening a file and sliding out several photos. 'Look,' he said, 'take a look at this, and if you tell me that this isn't a nobler building than the concrete sheds being offered to you, we will say no more. Well, what do you think?'

'You must be joking!' said Olivier and Christine together after looking at the pictures.

'No, I am absolutely serious.'

'But it's a ruin!' Olivier objected.

'No, it looks like a ruin, but that house dates back to a time when people were keen to construct something that would last, and last for centuries! The proof is that it dates back to 1620—witness the coats-of-arms decorating the two fireplaces.'

'Okay,' Olivier interrupted, 'but as there is no question of us throwing ourselves into the ruinous restoration of this monument, let's sign the papers for the plot we have decided on.'

'Fine,' said Maître Marsac. But then he added 'No regrets?'

'No.'

'But why did you want to sell us that one?' asked Christine.

'Because I thought you deserved to have a nice house, a real house. Once it is restored, this one will be magnificent...'

'Perhaps,' said the young woman, 'but why that house especially?'

'That's a good question,' said Maître Marsac, with a smile. 'That house and I have...a sentimental connection...Yes, the responsibility and rights of the sale of the property have belonged to my family since 1840. It was my great-great-grandfather who first had the task of selling that house. And here am I, one hundred and sixty-five years later, with it to sell again! It's my turn to find buyers who will bring it back to life. I should have liked you to have it. And, believe me, I am not trying to get rid of it. I should even go so far as to say that doing it up, plus the half-hectare of ground, will scarcely cost more than the current plan you find so attractive! And see how beautiful, how elegant it is.'

'It's all very well to say that,' Olivier remarked, looking again at the photos, 'but the roof must let in by the bucketful, for one thing, and as for the walls, I don't even dare think about them!'

'You are wrong. Everything is in a much better state than you might think. You would soon tell if you went and looked at it.'

'Is it really 1620s?' asked Christine.

'Yes, Madame. I know that, thanks to the departmental archives which have a record of the first owners. And it is because I know it so well that I do not want to sell it to just anyone. I should like it to have as much of a future as it has a past. I should like the stones to have more centuries of happiness, work, love, children's laughter, life to remember...'

'But why is it in such a bad state?' Olivier interjected.

'I'll explain. But first let me tell you the history. Well, it was built at the beginning of the seventeenth century by Engueyrant du Pibole de la Serbe, a councillor for the tribunal at Brive-la-Gaillarde. This man possessed a vast property, a huge fortune, which explains the size of the house and the luxurious Renaissance fireplaces, its porch, the uprights of the doors and columned windows, everything you can make out on the photos ... The building remained in the family of Pibole de la Serbe until 1840. But in the meantime one of the descendants of the first owner had become a thorough revolutionary. A radical who, in order to keep up with the current fashion, mangled his name and changed it to the simple Pierre Laserbe. Unfortunately for him, by dint of wanting to rid himself of his nobility and become a friend of the *sans-culottes*, he lost his head. It was a frequent occurrence after 1792 ... He had two daughters; the elder inherited but never married. On her death in 1810 the inheritance passed to one of her nephews and whereas his great-uncle had denied his origins, the nephew was proud of *his*, which, on his father's side, were lost in the mists of time. He was called Charles de Laroque du Grival, had an illustrious career in the army, and was made a general. That was a very sumptuous period for this fine house. Unfortunately our dashing young soldier became widowed and childless two years after he had got married.

He was 40 years old. Everything began to go downhill after that. Without anyone directly in line to inherit, the estate was divided between three of his great-nieces when he died. They split it up and sold everything that could be sold, including the house, of course. That's how my lawyer ancestor came to sell it to a big landowner. He left it to his son, a terrible fool of a man, lazy as a toad, who, after he had squandered almost all his fortune, decided one day he only needed one room to live in—he wasn't married—and that all the rest might as well be a cowshed and a hayloft. And the fool even put feeding-troughs in the Renaissance fireplaces! I told you this house had a terrible history!'

'Which explains its dreadful state,' said Olivier.

'Yes. In short, when the frightful dimwit died childless, some distant cousins inherited. They wanted to sell, of course, but could not agree amongst themselves. They fell out very bitterly and the house carried on deteriorating through lack of upkeep. That lasted forty years and only in the last two years has one single, sole proprietor put it into my hands. That's the reason I say this house has a soul, a past. That is also why I should have liked to see you take it on. With you it would have come back to life again, for generations to come...'

'What do you mean?' asked Christine.

'It's quite simple, Madame. You already have a son, and soon you will have another child and they will succeed you. As you have seen, this house lived its real, true life as long as there were children there to bring it alive and make it a good place to live in. And then one day, when there was no more children's laughter, it more or less ceased to breathe, to exist, it lost its soul. And I would very much have liked you to be the ones to give it back that soul. Listen, I can bring the price down a bit, the seller only wants to get rid of it, he lives in the United States you know. Yes, if you were to buy it I could get hold of some real artisans, very good ones, craftsmen. They will put it into excellent shape for you. But still, if you are not interested...'

'Well...' Olivier murmured, looking at his wife who was again deep in contemplation of the photographs.

'After all, darling,' she said, it doesn't cost us anything to go and see it... Maître Marsac is right, it has the charm of an old house, memories, a soul as well...'

'Go and see it?' said Olivier, after a moment's thought and looking at Maître Marsac. 'When?'

'Straight away if you like,' said the lawyer decisively.

'Let's go!'

Oliver and Christine Laborde and their children would be delighted to have your company at a house-warming, to celebrate the rehanging of the trammels, which should never have left the fire-places, constructed in the reign of Louis XIII by Engueyrant du Pibole de la Serbe, the builder of their new, but very old house...

A Mother's Tale

Guy de Maupassant

Meeting people is one of the joys of travel. We all know how delightful it is when, quite by chance, hundreds of miles from home, we bump into somebody from Paris, an old school friend, or someone who comes from our part of the world. Who has not passed a sleepless night in a little stagecoach jingling its way across the country, where steam travel is still unknown, seated next to some unknown young woman glimpsed in the beam of the lantern as she stepped on board the coach outside a whitewashed house in a country town?

And when morning comes, and your brains and ears are numbed by the constant tintinnabulation and the rattling of the windows, how delightful to see your pretty, tousled, travelling companion open her eyes, look about her, tidy her rebellious curls with the tips of her elegant fingers, and adjust her hair, ascertaining with a sure touch if her corset is straight, the waist in place and her skirts not too creased!

She looks at you too, one glance, cool and curious. Then she settles back in her corner apparently preoccupied solely with contemplating the countryside.

Yet you can't help observing her, you can't help your mind dwelling on her. Who is she? Where does she come from? Where is she going? In spite of yourself you sketch out a novella in your mind. She is pretty; she looks charming! Happy the man who . . . Would life be paradise with her by your side? Who knows? Perhaps she is the one to answer your needs, your dreams, your desires.

But how delicious, too, the disappointment when she gets out at the gate of a country dwelling. A man is there, waiting with two children and two maids. He takes her into his arms and kisses her as he sets her on the ground. She leans and takes up the little ones who are holding their arms out to her. She caresses them lovingly. And they all disappear up the path while the maids take the packages thrown down from the top of the coach by the driver.

Adieu! It is over. We shall never see her again. Farewell to the young woman who has spent the night at our side.

We do not know her, we have not spoken to her. Yet we are a little sad she has gone. Adieu!

I have so many of these travellers' tales, both happy and sad.

I was in the Auvergne, wandering on foot in those lovely French mountains that are not too high, not too demanding, but friendly and familiar. I had climbed the Sancy and I was going into a little inn near a pilgrim's chapel they call Notre Dame de Vassivière when I noticed an odd and rather comical elderly lady eating alone at a table at the back.

She was at least 70, tall, withered, angular, with white hair in tight, old-fashioned curls on her forehead. She was dressed like an English lady traveller, in a droll, untidy fashion, like someone who is quite indifferent to her appearance. She was eating an omelette and drinking water.

There was something strange about her, she looked anxious, it was the face of someone whom life has not treated kindly. I kept looking at her despite myself, wondering 'Who is she? What is her life like? What is she doing wandering around these mountains on her own?'

She paid and then got up to leave, pulling a funny little shawl round her shoulders, the two ends dangling over her arms. From a corner she took a long staff branded with many names and then she strode off, stiff and straight, like a postman with no time to waste.

A guide was waiting for her at the door. They disappeared. I watched them go down the valley along a path marked out by a line of large wooden crosses. She was taller than her companion and seemed to be outstripping him.

Two hours later I was climbing up the edge of the deep crater in which there lies, in a marvellous, enormous green hollow full of trees, brambles, rocks and flowers, the lake of Pavin, so round you would think it had been drawn with compasses, so clear and blue that you would believe it was a pool of azure that had flowed down from the sky, so delightful that it made you wish to live in a hut on the side of that wood above the crater in which the calm, cold water lay sleeping.

She was there, standing quite still, contemplating the clear expanse of water at the bottom of the dormant volcano. She was looking at it as though she was looking *into* it, into the unknown depths, populated, so they say, by monstrously big trout which have devoured all the other fish. As I passed by her, I thought I saw tears in her eyes. But she went striding off to rejoin her guide who had remained in an *estaminet* at the bottom of the ascent that leads to the lake.

I did not see her again that day.

The next day, as night was falling, I arrived at the Château de Murol. This ancient fortress, a gigantic tower standing on a peak in the middle of a wide valley where three smaller valleys meet, rises up against the sky, brown, cracked and falling to pieces, but very round, from its wide circular base to its little crumbling turrets at the top.

More than any other ruin it surprises you by its stark simplicity, its majesty, its imposing, ancient, gravity. There it is, standing on its own, as high as a mountain, like a dead queen, but a queen nonetheless of the valleys lying at her feet. You go up through a sloping plantation of fir trees, and at the top you enter by a narrow door and stop under the walls, in the first *enceinte*, with the whole countryside way down below.

Inside are rooms gone to rack and ruin, tumbledown staircases, secret crannies, underground passages, *oubliettes*, walls broken in the middle, arches still held up by a miracle, a labyrinth of stones, crevices in which grass grows and creatures crawl.

I was wandering round this ruin all on my own.

Suddenly, behind a length of wall, I saw a creature, a sort of ghost, like the spirit of this old, ruined place. I was startled. I was almost afraid. Then I recognized the elderly woman I had already met twice before.

She was weeping. Handkerchief in hand, she was weeping bitter tears. I turned to leave. She spoke to me, ashamed at having been discovered.

'Yes, Monsieur, I am weeping. A thing I do not often do.'

I stammered out something, not knowing what to say: 'I am sorry to have troubled you, Madame. You have no doubt been struck by some misfortune.'

She murmured: 'Yes . . . no—I am like a lost sheep.'

And putting her handkerchief to her eyes, she sobbed. I took her hands, trying to calm her, affected myself by her tears.

And then she blurted out her story, as if not to have to bear her sorrow all alone.

'Oh! . . . Oh! . . . Monsieur. If you only knew . . . how distressed I am . . . how distressed . . . I was happy . . . I have a house . . . over there . . . my home. I cannot go back there any more; I'll never go back again. It's too hard.

'I have a son . . . It's him! It's him! Children don't realize . . . Life is so short! If I could see him now, perhaps I should not even recognize him! How I loved him! Even before he was born, when I felt him move inside me. And then afterwards. How I kissed him, caressed him, cherished him! If you knew how many nights I spent watching him sleep, how many nights I spent thinking about him. I was devoted to him.

'He was 8 when his father sent him away to boarding school. It was over. He was no longer mine. Oh God! He came back to me on Sundays but that was all.

'Then he went to school in Paris. He only came back four times a year; and each time I was astonished by the change in him; by finding he had grown taller without me having seen him grow up. They stole his childhood from me, his trust, his love which would never have left me, all my delight in watching him grow up and become a young man.

'I saw him four times a year! Just imagine! At each visit his body, his expression, his movements, his voice, his laugh were no longer the same, were no longer mine. A child changes so quickly. And when you are not there to see him change, it is so sad. He is lost to you for good.

'One year he came back with down on his face! My son! I was dumbfounded . . . and sad, would you believe it? I hardly dared kiss him. Was it really him? My little boy, my blond, curly-headed little boy, my darling child that I had held on my knees as a baby, who had drunk my milk with his greedy little lips, this tall dark young man who could no longer kiss me, who seemed to love me mostly out of a sense of duty, who respectfully called me 'mother' and kissed me on the forehead when I would have wished to hold him tightly in my arms?

'My husband died. Then it was my parents' turn. Then I lost my two sisters. When death enters a house you might suppose he is in a hurry to get through all the tasks he can so that he won't have to come back again for a long time. He leaves one or two people alive, to mourn the rest.

'I was alone. My son had grown up and was studying law. I hoped to live and die near to him. I went to join him so that we could live together. He had adopted the habits of a young man. He gave me to understand that I was in his way. I left. I was wrong to do so. But I was suffering too much through feeling that I, his mother, was not wanted. I returned home.

'After that I hardly saw him at all.

'He got married. How wonderful! Were we finally going to be united for ever? I should have grandchildren! He had married an Englishwoman who took a strong dislike to me. Why? Did she perhaps feel that I loved him too much? I was forced to go away again. I found myself alone. Yes, monsieur.

'Then he left for England. He was going to live with *them*, with his wife's people. Do you understand? They have him to themselves—my son! They have stolen him from me! He writes to me every month. He used to come and see me at first. Now he does not come any more.

'I haven't seen him for four years! His face was lined and his hair white. How could this be? That old man my son? The little pink-cheeked baby I once had? I suppose I shall never see him again.

'And so I go travelling all year long. I wander around in every direction, as you see, all alone.

'I am like a lost sheep. Farewell, monsieur, don't stay, it pains me that I have told you all this.'

And as I went down the hill again, I turned to see the elderly woman standing on a broken wall, gazing out at the mountains, the long valley and Lake Chambon in the distance. And her skirts and the funny little shawl that she was wearing on her thin shoulders were billowing out around her like pennants in the wind.

The Bull from Jouvet

Paul Hervieu

On the Grande Côte, where no trees have ever been able to grow, Hugues Barros keeps two hundred sheep, and owns a quarter of them.

In the three months since Easter he has been moving his animals up to the remote pastures he has rented for the summer between the mont des Archets, Combelouve, les Bains de l'Ours and the lake of Jouvet.

Today he's expecting his weekly provisions. Last week's are finished and he is hungry.

Before him he has the slow-moving mass of his flock. There are a few brown fleeces in among the white woolly backs.

214 ■ Paul Hervieu

Hugues Barros stands leaning his tall frame on a sturdy staff of holly, whose bark he has ringed with his knife. His strong shoulders fill out the large cavalry greatcoat he bought last winter from a pedlar selling ex-army uniforms in the markets. When the north wind lifts this ample covering and flattens it against the hollow of his back, his brown cord trousers are visible, twisted in thick leather garters. The shepherd's rough peasant face is protected by a wide-brimmed felt hat scorched by the sun, streaked by the dust and the rain.

Hugues frequently consults the sky to find out the time, and is becoming impatient, aware of his insides crying out for food.

At last his two dogs come closer and growl, and prick up their ears.

He places his calloused hand on his forehead, to shade it, and spies his wife climbing very slowly up the combe of Nant-Gelé.

La Barros is carrying a capacious basket on her left arm, and with her right hand she is pulling along a scrawny bull with short legs. One of its horns is broken and the other is flattened and black at the tip.

From time to time, with a simple backwards jerk of his head, the brute causes the woman leading him to stop, and runs his purple tongue complacently over his dark flank.

'Get a move on!' the shepherd yells.

But his wife, her throat constricted by the climb, makes no answer.

Again he shouts:

'What you got there? Where'd that animal come from?'

When la Barros gets to the top she hastens to answer him, breathing hard:

'It's that mangy beast's made me late. You got to look after him on Tayot's account, while he's in rut...He won't stay in the field nor he won't stay in the shed.'

'How much will Tayot give me for my trouble?'

'He said he'll make it right with you later.'

'Oh yeah, well you can tell him I want at least twenty sous a week. I have to pay ninety francs for my lodgings here.'

'I'll tell him.'

While his wife is unpacking her basket the man goes to fetch a pick and a mallet from his stone hut, and he hammers the bull's rope in the ground a few yards away. The bull observes him, sly and motionless, with bloodshot eyes.

When Hugues comes back and sits down against a hummock he takes pleasure in surveying his provisions spread out on the bare ground where the wind is curling the few tufts of grass.

Good. This time the cottage loaf was a good size. The blue cheese, of cow's and goat's milk, was just right too...And the bacon? Where was that then? She had forgotten it! Bloody women!...

But wait a moment! La Barros smiles. Here is the bacon and the sausage and tobacco and the two litres of local wine to sharpen the taste of the water from the spring.

The shepherd sets to and rapidly assuages his appetite, chatting with his mouth full. Are the children all right? The eldest has been up to his tricks again. He'll be a right one. The lasses had better watch out! What about father? He still won't have the operation on the gland in his throat? He'll choke one of these days. Well, we've told him plenty of times! So the *garde champêtre* has decided to bring a charge against Joseph Mabre's geese. Well he had it coming! And that powder for his gun that the carrier was supposed to be bringing back from Albertville, when was it arriving? Because since last night a couple of vultures have been flying round the Grand Rey where a lamb had fallen...

Hugues Barros has finished his frugal meal. He unscrews the wooden cork of the wineskin he carries on his shoulder. Raising the goatskin with both hands he squeezes a thin, cool jet of wine on to his tongue.

Then, smoothing his moustache, he leans over his wife and makes love to her, as is right and natural, without the necessity of hiding from anyone.

While la Barros, relieved of her burden, goes down the slopes to the village of Longefoy again with a light, firm step, her husband, lying replete on his belly, draws thick puffs of smoke from his black pipe.

For a week, no doubt, he will not see another human face . . . But what does he care! . . .

Beneath his half-closed lids he sees in the valley of Aime the Isère, cutting straight through the woods and rocks like the blade of a knife. The houses of Centron, standing among the trees of an ancient forest, look like yellow butterflies in a hedge of briar-roses. The vines of Bellentre way down below carpet the land in a mossy green.

When the shepherd turns his face on the pillow he has made with his arms, he sees, at the bottom of the mountain opposite, the green lakes in the val de Tignes which resemble long drinking-troughs into which waterfalls are cascading like the manes of white horses.

At last he dozes off into a heavy and dreamless midday sleep.

Suddenly he is woken by the barking of his dogs. The bull, with a violent effort, has uprooted his post and is dragging it, sowing panic among the rams and the sheep in-lamb.

'After that bull!...Sic 'im, sic, sic!...' cries Hugues Barros, waving his arms furiously.

But the dogs, unused to such orders, stay where they are, howling and refusing to move.

'Wait, you mangy creature, I'll see to you!'

And he walks towards the bull.

Boldly, the bull stops short and lowers his menacing, mutilated forehead.

Barros hits him on the nose with his mallet. And as soon as the bull has turned aside with a bellow he takes the tether in his fist. Then, one-handed, he bangs in the stake once more, fetches some heavy stones and places them along the length of the rope, so that the beast's nostrils are right down touching the surface of the earth.

'You can starve for a bit,' he said, 'that'll calm you down.'

And he lets loose one blow after another on the animal's spine.

Then he leads his flock to a new pasture.

The animals, crowding together, nose out the close-cropped roots of what remains of the grass and move away. And while the dogs are harrassing them, their hasty cloven feet rip apart the red or blue corollas of the foxgloves, wolfsbane and all the poisonous flowers which, ravenous though they are, they avoid.

...As evening approaches, Hugues comes back with his sheep and settles them, some clambering on the backs of others, in between a giant rock and three small fences.

But the one-horned beast has again found a means of escape. He is wandering around, snuffling at the breeze, uttering sporadic bellows, whipping his flanks with the bristly end of his long and supple tail.

The stupefied shepherd mutters between his teeth:

'So, that's what you want, do you, you piece of scum? Well you've got it coming to you!'

And he runs at him again, with his cudgel hanging at his elbow by the strap.

The bull, who is waiting, as if he has made up his mind, scrabbles at the earth with his hoof and kicks up clods. Then, at the moment when he might fight back, his shifty eyes move and with one sideways jump he shies away down the valley of Armene.

Hugues Barros follows. And there ensues a furious chase across the escarpments of schist, the residues of snow, the screes and the running water.

Only once near the ruined barn of les Blancs did the man catch up with the animal. He tried to seize it from behind by the horns and bring it down as he had learned to do, by twisting its neck. But on one side of the bull's head his hand encountered only a stump and an ear. He hung on nonetheless, kicking the backs of his adversary's legs with his iron toe-caps. The bull, who had the advantage of only one horn, jumped free and disappeared into the darkness which had at last risen from the plains.

Barros, who has rolled into a quagmire, curses him as he gets to his feet:

'Go to hell!'

His hands and his grazed knees are bleeding and smarting. In the oncoming darkness he gets his bearings by one last ray of light and espies the plateau on which his hut is perched. Painfully he manages to get back to the Grande Côte. But as soon as he reaches it, he is alarmed by a powerful galloping noise...

A shape, darker than the surrounding blackness, charges at him. And without even time to utter one cry he falls backwards and passes out, his chest pierced by the bull's single horn.

When he regains consciousness, the round moon is high in the heavens. The circle of glaciers round about is bathed in its clear and liquid brightness. And from the col du Soufre to the Mont-Pourri by way of Gebroulaz, the Grande Casse and the Iseran, the surface of the snow shines like a flora of sparks spread upon flower beds of crystal.

Hugues Barros is extremely cold.

He tries to get up, but the movement causes an agonizing pain in the pit of his stomach. And when he puts his hand to it, it is sticky, and as far as he can see, reddish and oozing.

Then he remembers what has happened.

He lets out a sigh and then a groan. He feels wounded in his innermost being and the solitude makes him afraid in a way he has never been before. His entire body shakes with fever and visions pass before his eyes. Mont-Blanc, opposite him, seems to reach up as high as the moon and on its slopes the Allée Blanche and the Glacier des Glaciers are dancing.

He utters a wild cry. His broken voice sounds frightening to him as it falls into the emptiness and total silence. The sheep and dogs are all asleep.

Slowly the night passes and vanishes gradually into the dawn.

The sun rises beneath its triumphal arch of supernatural colours, golden blue, pearl red, flame grey.

Dazzled by the light, Barros tries to steal a look at his wound and satisfy his terrible curiosity. He is suffering dreadfully. His solution is to press his fists over the gaping wound. And by this expense of strength his pain is momentarily relieved. His blood, congealed on the grass, glistens and mixes with the white frost. He is consumed by a burning thirst. But he cannot reach his gourd that has been thrown beneath his back during his fall.

The dogs, however, surprised at his unaccustomed lateness, set up a chorus of barking. And the hungry sheep, pushing back their insubstantial enclosure, escape in a bleating mass into the fresh grass. And before long the flock will be nothing but an almost invisible dot disappearing in the direction of les Frasses.

Soon the shepherd hears the harsh plaintive noise of the rutting bull a short distance away. He is not alarmed by his return. On the contrary, he wishes the animal would charge at him again and finish him off. Otherwise how long will he take to die, writhing in pain like a man condemned?

... But then suddenly he becomes anxious—is something going on down below? ...

A group of people are getting down from their mules and ascending the final cone of Le Jouvet on foot. Four men and two women in light-coloured clothing.

Barros can see their shapes quite clearly outlined against the sky, their arms pointing with spyglasses at the great contours of the landscape.

He is frustrated, for no one is looking in his direction. And he feels sorry for himself as the vast shadow of these people, who had so very nearly reached him, retreats into the distance.

He implores them weakly with gestures and cries. All efforts are in vain. The tourists leave without seeing him and only the bull answers him with lamentations of his own.

'Murder them as well, you bastard,' he mutters.

He thinks about his misfortune.

He has never had much luck. Not that he has had a lot to complain about...But the events of his life pass through his mind. He especially recalls the time he was obliged to leave the army and the hours during which his three children were born...He also remembers the calm face of one of his neighbours whom he had seen die, surrounded by his nearest and dearest.

The day advances. The sun is behind the clouds.

Dense fog enters France through the usual route of the Petit-Saint-Bernard, condenses and approaches the slopes of the Grande Côte and there begins its endless procession, hymned by the wind.

Hugues Barros can no longer see anything on this earth. A slight foam rises through the corners of his mouth, frequent spasms shake his limbs. With one last effort he raises himself little by little into a sitting position.

And he dies sitting up, his eyes vague, like a creature that is just awakening.

We Can't Go On Like This

Anne-Marie Garat

Why did I take that minor road instead of the main road that morning? Who can say what really happened? In the driver's mirror I can see my face—the face of a stranger; he knows the whole story but is saying nothing. Perhaps it was only something he dreamed up, something wicked, savage. Bad thoughts, evil thoughts, course through the brain at night; you forget them but they come back a long time after, from another life. I wonder why I took that by-road one morning in October.

The petrol station was set back among the trees and ferns, I glimpsed it only for an instant out of the corner of my eye as I drove past. I wasn't going very fast. But actually I didn't see the petrol station or the house or anything except the 'For Sale' sign attached to the petrol pump. I very nearly missed it. In which case I wouldn't have stopped. And nothing would have happened.

I was driving mechanically, in that state where you let images float in and out of your head, like a film running sleepily behind the windscreen. I was lulled by the steady noise of the engine and the monotony of the landscape. There were swathes of mist on the road, white drifts that I tore and that closed again behind me. I jammed on the brakes without thinking. When I came to a halt, I woke and looked in the driving mirror. There was nothing behind me but the empty misty road that I had been mindlessly following for so many kilometres. I might have been any-where. So, just to check, I put the car in reverse and backed slowly for a couple of hundred metres till I was exactly level with the sign. 'For Sale'. I pulled in onto the verge, put the car in neutral, and left the engine running. I only wanted a quick look.

It was an autumn morning. There was this thin mist, sparkling gently, sticking to the ferns and hanging among the trees as well. All around, the immense pine forest, damp after the night, spread out, blue and russet red. Not many landscapes are like this: dead straight forest roads running for ten or twenty kilometres without a bend; or if they bend, they run for another ten or twenty straight to the next village, to the back of beyond. Village, if you can call it that. The sign indicates you are approaching a populated area, but in fact it's nothing but a vague clearing with a few isolated buildings, low farmhouses with large tiled roofs scattered here and there among the trees, no church spire, no village shop, nothing. You drive straight through without slowing down and that's how the gendarmes get you on your way out. They know where to position themselves. Nothing's more lonely than these forest roads cut across at intervals by narrow grassy, sandy tracks disappearing into the distance, out of which may come a man on a scooter or a tractor carrying loggers. On these roads you can fall asleep with your eyes wide open, in this interminable, wild, lonely countryside. That's perhaps why I took the old road that morning, instead of the expressway, which gets you to the coast in two hours. I certainly needed some sleep, even the eyes-wide-open sort, after the sleepless night I had just spent listening to my wife. And then I suddenly saw the petrol station.

It was off the road, camouflaged by pines, squashed in amongst the tall ferns. A shack put together out of concrete blocks and planks, painted blue and green and, to judge by the state it was in, certainly not painted at all for several years. The breeze-blocks were crumbling, the cracks had been filled in with rough plaster mixed with filings. The most recent colour must have been pine green, which meant that the house melted into the background and I might well have gone past without noticing it. But it had turned a greenish-grey and was flaking off, uncovering streaks of colour that were older: you might imagine the building only remained standing by virtue of its layers of paint. And yet, if you half shut your eyes, from the other side of the road, through your eyelashes, you could tell that the petrol station must have been a fine sight in its day, with its tiled canopy roof in the style of the region, and decorated with a lacy, but now wormeaten, wood frieze. The sign was still on its pediment, the 'Mobil Oil' logo with its famous winged red horse half worn away. In front of the door, on a petrol pump that had come loose but was still standing, hung the 'For Sale' sign, a kind you don't see any more except on old posters or in Edward Hopper pictures. It had a round top shaped like a clock without hands. It must once have been red. The other two pumps were lying against the walls of the shack among a pile of old iron, rotting rags, and old tyres. Their bases remained in the concrete in front of the house with grass and brambles growing up around them.

I turned off the engine and all at once there was total silence. I lit a cigarette. I can't deny that the ghost of an idea was stirring at the back of my head, but it was very vague. I let it float around. In the absolute silence I drew at leisure on my cigarette looking at the ruined shack painted in old green, with its old red pump and the forest behind, the orange ferns, the white mist around like milk. It all felt very quiet and abandoned, like in a dream. Behind the petrol station, at the back, I could see a wooden building, a sort of shed, like a workshop or a garage for a tractor, with rotting doors barricaded with planks of wood, half-collapsed beneath brambles. The funniest thing was that it was for sale. Someone must have thought this ruin might appeal to somebody. And the funniest thing was, that somebody could well be me that morning. I began to laugh. We can't go on like this, my wife had said last night and other nights before. That was my opinion too, but words are deceptive and I'm not sure we both meant the same thing. Probably we did not agree about that either.

I got out of the car. The door closed softly behind me, a very peaceful noise. There was nothing on the road to right or left; as far as my eyes could see, everything was deserted, silent. Opposite me was the petrol station. And I was all alone. It was a long time since I had felt so alone, so calm, all by myself. It was a long time since I had stopped suddenly in a place for no particular reason. I had all the time in the world. I had left home far too early, having scarcely swallowed down my boiling hot coffee.

I stayed in the shower for ages, I knew she was waiting for me in the kitchen. I thought we were going to 'go on like that' yet again. But no, she was in her pyjamas, leaning against the kitchen sink, sniffing. She was dabbing at the end of her nose with a tissue, glancing at me covertly, not speaking. I burned my mouth with the coffee.

'See you tonight, Nad, don't worry,' I said quietly, giving her a kiss on her forehead.

I was expecting her to fend me off, but she didn't.

'It's going to rain. Take care on the road,' she said, kindly.

This piece of advice was somewhat unexpected after the things she had been throwing at me all night. But Nad has considerable reserves of energy. In spite of her Lexomil tablets and her sleeping pills, she is ready for battle all night. She can come out with the most horrible sneers, reproaches, and insults, and puts her heart into her weeping and her vicious remarks. Then at the very moment you think she must be emptied, exhausted, she goes back to holding a normal conversation, as though nothing had occurred. You might have thought she had forgiven me for the sleepless night we had just gone through because of her. I made no attempt to seek any explanation for this recovery of sympathy. I left, taking good care not to slam the door behind me. That's the kind of thing she is capable of brooding over for a whole day and moans about when

I come in, as if I had just left her. Nad's got like that, she can't put up with a thing any more. She has no appetite for anything, myself included, and we don't know what we can do to get out of it. We hurt each other, as soon as we are closeted together in the house. Though we are not children, we need someone to separate us, to decide for us that enough is enough.

From behind the kitchen window she watched me cross the garden and get the car out of the garage; she gave me a little wave, and I waved too and had a momentary impulse to go back and kiss her again, but what would be the point? I said to myself: perhaps it's the house that isn't right. We must leave, go and live somewhere else, find a place to start again, become people nobody knows. I crossed the estate slowly, it was off-to-school time. Neighbours' children with nagging mothers were piling into cars. We don't have any children. Luckily, as a pretext for leaving early in the morning I can say I have clients to visit, because in the state we were in that morning I think we should have gone mad. My clients come in very handy but actually, my first appointment was at midday, 200 kilometres away. I had plenty of time. That's what must have made me take the old road at the last moment.

It's not often you find yourself in the middle of the forest early in the morning. When you live in a town, in the end you forget what that's like. There was a crispness in the October air, a wafting of nature's scents, resin, humus, and no noise. I crossed the road. The shutters were well and truly shut. The door likewise, nailed up with planks. I started to daydream about this house that was for sale. I am not much of a handyman, but I'd be able to renovate it pretty cheaply with a bit of plaster and cement...

'The place is too near the road,' I said to myself. 'Although, if I pulled out the pump and the broken concrete blocks, if I dug it all up and put in a good-sized hedge... What would that be?... Let's see now, eight or ten metres from the side of the road, that's not so bad. There can't be anyone passing. Nobody much, anyway. A good hedge of broom, hawthorn, a natural camouflage of brambles; no one could see you, no one would know you were there behind all that...'

I was telling myself this little tale, for no real reason, without really believing it. A cosy little house in the woods for the odd weekend. It was a place where you could go hunting, I could get a permit—not for shooting: guns and animals, I'm not interested in such things. But to have a bit of peace and quiet. Nad loathes the country, says that nature makes her feel depressed. I'd buy a gun, and a shooting permit just to have a bit of peace from time to time in my hut hidden in the woods. I'd make fires, get myself something to eat, listen to the kind of music I like, read a good book. Sci-fi, that's all I read. This new idea tickled my fancy and made me laugh. My curiosity even made me walk as far as the corner of the wall into the wet ferns under the pines. And there, surprise surprise, was an immaculate little vegetable patch with a well, both invisible from the road. I just had time to turn round and I was face to face with him.

'Private property,' he said, sending a brown gob of spit to the side.

He must have come silently out of the back door of his house. He was small, about 60, dry as a stick, neat and cleanshaven, with eyes like pale blue glass.

'I was just passing,' I said defensively, 'I saw the sign.'

'Did you now?' he remarked gloomily, putting away his penknife.

'There's a "For Sale" sign, isn't there?'

He hiccoughed, or it might have been a laugh.

'OK,' I said, 'OK. Sorry to disturb you.'

'That depends, doesn't it,' he said, sending out another jet of saliva.

He scrutinized me, through half-closed eyelids. I must say that in my loden and my town clothes, I didn't look like someone who was an amateur of petrol stations.

'Do you live here?' I asked.

I was only being polite, because my one thought now was to escape. The sudden appearance of this little guy on the scene had brought me back to the real world.

'Been here forty years, huh.'

'Quiet, I should think.'

'Quiet, huh.'

I noticed that peculiar 'huh' he ended his sentences with; it wasn't a question. It came out of the back of his throat through his nose like the blow of an axe, a way of stopping his voice or interrupting himself, if you like.

I made as if to leave. He came a step or two with me.

'The sign,' he said, 'I hung it up two years ago. Nobody has stopped since. Not a bloody soul.'

'I never come this way, it's the first time,' I said by way of explanation.

'It's for sale, huh,' he said, clearing his throat after a silence.

'You shouldn't be surprised nobody stops. From the road it looks totally deserted.'

'That's deliberate, to have a bit of peace, so that nobody comes asking for petrol.'

'Ah yes, of course.'

While I hesitated, not knowing how to get out of the situation without being rude, he pointed at the house with his chin.

'Come in and have a look at least, huh. You may as well.'

At that point, I could not but accept. He might have got cross if his first customer had turned tail on him too quickly. He let me in, pushed back the shutters. We were in a large, low room, which had been the main room of the petrol station. The formica counter was still there, but he had put in what passed for a kitchen behind it and the shelves for the oil cans had been made into shelving for his pots and pans, the assorted jumble of someone living on his own who was very particular about cleanliness. The entire wall was windowless, with panelling which blocked the openings on the side that looked out on to the road. As for the rest, he had decorated it like a proper house, with a country clock, benches and table covered with an oilcloth, on which were laid a large loaf, a half-eaten sausage, and a bottle of red wine. I'd probably disturbed him while he was eating. There were some little rustic baubles: plates hung on the whitewashed wall, the Post Office calendar, a large barometer. In one corner there was a rustic bed, presumably it was his own, high, narrow, with sheets tucked in, army-fashion. A large, enamelled, cast-iron stove stood in splendour by the side of it, a Godin, of the kind you don't see any more.

'And this, as you can see,' he said, lifting a curtain, 'is the bedroom, huh.'

I glanced at it, slightly embarrassed at the turn of events, his manner of showing me round seemed serious. The shutters were closed, I espied in the half light a large oak bed, a massive cupboard, a rug, a sewing machine. Everything was tidy, frozen, covered in dust. No one had slept there for ages. It was a mortuary.

'Very nice,' I said, taking a step back. He remained a moment longer in the doorway, his arm raised, holding back the curtain, looking into the darkness. Then he dropped the curtain again.

We returned to the large room, lit up by the beautiful morning light. The astonishing thing was that once you were back in there you forgot everything, the road, the petrol pump, the abandoned, shabby exterior. It was like being on the other side of the globe, you had turned your back, you were miles away. Through the window panes and the open door all you could see was his small well-tended patch of garden with the blue forest stretching out behind, the gloomy colonnade of great pines drifting far away into the mist. A sleepy lethargy seemed to be entering me, it was as though I had just arrived somewhere. I had the strange feeling that I had just taken a decision. Or rather that I hadn't taken any decision, I was already engaged on something, things had taken their course without my intervention. As at other times when I woke in the middle of my life, suddenly much further away,

I wasn't sure when, but something had happened, had been decided without me.

'It's for sale,' he said. 'Everything. The furniture, the tools. The lot, huh.'

'Are you thinking of leaving?'

'You're interested, huh?'

I misunderstood his question.

'Not at all, it is as you please.'

'No,' he rectified patiently, 'does the house interest you?'

'Oh!... The house...'

I was taken aback, embarrassed.

'Yes, I like it a lot,' I said, all at once on an impulse. 'It's the kind of place I'm looking for.'

As far as 'looking for' was concerned, I was lying. But as to the rest, I was telling the truth, and I did like the place, despite its shabbiness.

'Not many people looking for this sort of place, huh.'

He looked at his house, hands on hips, and nodded. He was talking to himself.

'I'd stopped thinking anyone would come. If I'd thought that this morning! What a joke, huh.'

He tapped the side of his head with his palm.

'So you're not from this part of the world,' he went on.

'I'm from the town.'

'No, I mean, you're not from this country.'

'No, Portugal. My parents.'

He let out a big 'oh' of satisfaction or surprise, he was on the point of saying something, then he was silent, his mouth open. He gazed into space.

'That doesn't make any difference,' he said, giving himself a little shake. 'For the water, the pump is outside, you draw it from the well. As for the electricity, all you have to do is get reconnected. They cut me off a while back, I don't give a damn, I live with the sun and I've got my oil lamp. Same for the phone. But the line is there. All modern amenities, huh,' he concluded. 'The toilets are outside, the ones the customers used.'

He scratched the back of his neck. Then spat on the ground, politely, to one side.

'So it's yes, huh.'

'Listen,' I said with an effort. 'Not so fast. I need to think. I can't say yes or no that quickly.'

Suddenly he seemed so anxious I felt sorry for him. He looked at his nails, began to bite the skin around his thumb and pull it off, all the time glancing out of the window towards the bottom of the garden and the forest.

'You had no business to come then,' he said brusquely. 'Shouldn't lead people on, huh.'

'Oh come now, it's normal to want to think about it.'

'What do you need to think about? You can see straight away if you like it or not. Would you like a little glass of something?'

Without waiting for me to answer he took the cork out of the red wine and filled a mustard glass, putting it down among the breadcrumbs. We sat at the table on benches facing each other, he against the light, me in the light, and I had trouble seeing his face. Red wine in the morning is not part of my usual routine, but I didn't dare refuse. This neat little man with eyes like glass marbles was having a weird effect on me. He was making me feel sleepy. He reminded me of my father and yet he wasn't in the least like him, but I felt I had gone back in time several years to when my father had decided to return to Portugal, to his home country, with his meagre savings. That was when he acquired that hard, hunted look, the shifty look of a frightened child. He had worked like a slave for twenty-five years as a builder's labourer, mixing cement and building walls in all weathers. He knew nothing of the world except his work and family, my mother and me. People believe that the money foreigners earn they steal from them. I saw how together they went about putting aside their pennies all those years. They were in agreement about what they wanted: a new house in the village, they wanted to go back there with their little pot of gold and they thought I was going to go back with them, it seemed the natural thing to do. We never talked about it, but I had spent holidays two or three times in their godforsaken village after thirty hours riding in the bus, and it was

enough to last me a lifetime. And I hadn't won my scholarship at Business School for nothing. The result was that
we fell out. Before leaving, they cashed in the lot, sold it to
the dealers, to the neighbours, everything they possessed,
even the saucepans and my schoolbooks. They only had
one suitcase and the wad of their savings in a wallet. I didn't
go with them to the station. I didn't see them again.

'I'm Jo, huh,' he said, after clearing his throat noisily.

'Michel,' I said.

He held out his hand solemnly over our glasses. He was
smiling, his teeth yellowed and loosened by nicotine, but
he was smiling only with his mouth, not his eyes.

'It's not always been like this here, huh. I opened the
petrol station just after the war. It was a going concern at
that time. There was the American military base and all
the traffic going to the coast, the tourists going to the
beach. I had a wife. She was brave, she served petrol day
and night. We took it in turns. I also did a bit of mechanics, breakdowns. We even had a Citroën, a Traction
before that, huh. I paid off the loan in no time. The
whole place belongs to me here, there's no problem.
What else do you want to know?'

He was talking quickly now, the words were coming
thick and fast and his speech was slurred. He looked
straight at my tie. He stuffed a quid of tobacco into his
cheek.

'Things took a turn for the worse. The Yanks closed the base and quit. Because they saw US GO HOME scrawled on walls, obviously. Then they built the expressway, and that was that. Nobody, not a single customer. My wife got cancer. And that was that. My daughter went to live in the town. Apparently she sells dresses. I'd rather not know what she gets up to, it makes me feel sick. I shut the shop and sold the car. That was that. Now I've got my bit of pension.'

'And so you want to retire.'

'Right. Retire, huh.'

Time passed but I didn't care. You couldn't hear a thing, especially not cars. You would have thought you were deep in the woods. And everything seemed very remote to me, as though it belonged to another life—my wife, my clients, the sleepless night. As for buying his wretched shack, I wasn't there yet. I hadn't quite lost my senses. It was certain this poor old chap was imagining all sorts, getting all worked up about his sign. Who in the world today would buy his four walls made of breeze-blocks? But I felt like staying a bit longer, hypnotized, carried along by it all.

'With the money,' he continued, 'I'll be able to pay for a place at Les Oiseaux. Cosy and peaceful, huh.'

'Les Oiseaux?' I asked vaguely, just to keep the conversation going.

'The new council retirement home in town. I've found out about it. I put my money in the bank and they allocate me some each month. At Les Oiseaux they'll take me whenever I want with my bit of pension. With my savings. Just the job.'

'Oh,' I said, 'that's a good idea.'

'That's what I want to do, huh. I'm not so badly off here, but there are a few problems. I can't cope with the shopping now, fifteen kilometres on my moped, or all the hassle of the garden. In there you get waited on, they do your bed, give you personal care, whatever you need. So, have you made up your mind?'

'I'll have to see,' I said, with a slight shrug.

'A hundred thousand, huh,' he suddenly said, his eyes round as marbles in his thin, shadowy face.

I almost burst out laughing. A hundred thousand euros! The man must be round the bend! And then I realized he was talking old francs. Scarcely fifteen thousand euros he wanted, for his crummy petrol station and his pocket-handkerchief of a garden. A paltry sum. At that minute I was staggered at the figure he mentioned. Fifteen thousand euros. I could write a cheque straight away. Then my idea about a quiet spot for weekends came back to mind, but this time it was like a real object that I could touch, stroke at my leisure.

'It's just that you would like some little amenities in addition, huh. A few little things.'

Without talking to Nad about it, nor to anyone at all. A little place that was mine, all mine.

'Right, let's go. I'll show you a few little things, shall I?'

Meticulously he rinsed the glasses, swept the crumbs off the table and put the cork back in the bottle. He put on a fur-lined jacket and we went out. The sun was just coming through the mist, great slanting rays crossed the colonnade of pine trees and the dew was sparkling on his lettuces. He scrutinized me from head to toe.

'You're not exactly kitted out for walking, huh. We're going to walk a bit, will you be all right?'

'I'll be all right,' I said.

He locked the door. We plunged into the forest. I didn't look back. I felt happy, remote from everything, my life was rolling away at a great rate behind me, it did not exist, any more than a dream. I felt giddy, like on a children's roundabout.

We walked for a good while along a path between tall ferns, him first, me following, in silence. My trouser legs got wet straight away but I didn't care. The smell of the humus that had wafted towards me when I got out of my car hit me again, it came from everywhere, welling up in waves of freshness from under the ferns, from under the russet pine needles, that dulled our footfalls. Bare-headed and with my hands stuck into the pockets of my loden, I was ready to go anywhere, I wanted to see just how far. He left the path at one point and we cut through the wood, following a path he seemed to know like the back of his hand. A very clean forest, maintained by the forestry, with the undergrowth neatly trimmed. I walked with my head back, looking at the great branches high, high overhead, swaying in the wind, the lovely waves of murmuring wind. Then the ground began to slope downwards and we descended in sandy soil to a steep-sided valley, to a stream abundant with water that wound its peaceful, translucent way along, with little silver eddies between banks of red clay. You had to know the water course was there before you could find it. You would not have been able to guess at the natural dip from anywhere around.

Jo camped beside the river. His laugh resembled a hiccough.

'All you want of 'em here. Bleak, trout, even pike. Catch them with live bait, gudgeon, huh.'

He laughed out loud.

'And fresh water shrimps galore a bit further up there in the crack in the rocks, believe you me. And frogs if you care for them, huh.'

And he turned to me rubbing his hands, and spitting to one side.

'The price suits you, huh.'

I kept a straight face. Rather. But I wasn't going to tell him so straight away. Now I entered into the game, pretending to be difficult so that he would lead me on wherever he wanted. I wanted him to tempt me still, I felt he had other things to show me.

'They call it La Leyrette, this stream. It winds down to the lake that way. A good kilometre, huh. My wife,' he went on abruptly, 'was from Portugal, like you. From Faro. You must know it, huh.'

'No, we come from the north. Faro's in the south.'

'Oh.'

He seemed disappointed. So I said:

'It's a lovely part of the country, I believe.'

The 'we' which had come from nowhere had stuck in my throat. It's the kind of remark I never make and I wished I hadn't.

'They say it's lovely, but poor, huh. She came over with her father, a seasonal worker, when they started planting maize. They started acting like Americans, cutting down the forest round here to plant maize, fields of it as far as you could see. They needed workers. A beautiful woman, huh. We got married. Then she got cancer and that was that.'

At that moment we heard an explosion, a muffled shot from a gun somewhere. But the report rang out above our heads for some time, amplified in the silence.

'Bloody hell!'

He blinked and his glassy eyes were like slits. He looked straight towards the place the shot had come from, seeming even to know its exact distance from us.

'Bastards,' he said. 'The shooting season only opens on Sunday. They have two days a year for the deer, and that's all. It makes them mad. They're at it already. They say it's to get them moving. The bastards.'

Angrily, he spat to one side.

'Come on, let's go. I'll show you something else, huh.'

We retraced our steps. As we walked he attempted to point out some markers so that I could memorize the way we had come. A copse of green oaks, a bush of broom, a little clearing, but I had been lost for quite some while, time passed and I didn't in the least care. We reached a place that was more grassy, with sparse crimson ferns below the little oaks. I couldn't see any difference, the whole forest looked the same.

'There,' he said, throwing his arms out. 'This is my own special place. Private property. Secret, huh. On your left, the girolles. On your right, the ceps. Come and see.'

He went through the motions of looking round his feet whereas I, knowing nothing about it, could see them without even looking, the little beige and orange girolles standing up like bunches of flowers. He picked a handful of them and held them out to me to smell. While I was burying my nose in the fleshy mushrooms, with their fresh, grassy scent, he was laughing silently and looking hard at me. He winked suddenly.

'You like that, huh?'

I silently agreed. Suddenly he frowned.

'You don't hunt, do you?'

I shook my head. I had no intention of telling him about my plan for the gun and the shooting permit now.

'That's good. Because as far as I'm concerned, people who go shooting, huh...'

He made a sign with the edge of his hand as if he were cutting his throat. Then he added with another wink:

'You need more than that, for the same price?'

I laughed. I said:

'Yes, more for the same price.' He laughed too.

'Come on, let's go.'

We walked on. We crossed rays of sun and patches of shade. Two or three times an animal made a bolt for it somewhere in the ferns, something took off over our heads. As it did so, Jo would say without turning his head:

'Hare. Partridge. Pheasant.'

I could see nothing at all, except the narrow path, along which we were making good progress. I was soaked to my knees, my feet were starting to get cold, but I would not for all the world have complained. I was full of a gaiety filled with nostalgia. After a long detour he slowed down, Indian-style, and we reached the top of a large combe, where there was a vast sunken bowl in the forest. From there you could see below the trees a sort of flowery hollow of briars, pink and purple, and tall clumps of ferns burnt a copper colour by the sun. He made a sign to me not to move, and whispered:

'There... Look. On the edge of the thicket, huh.'

Then I saw them. Three young roe deer with small, fair antlers, busy grazing, like animals from ancient, medieval tales, proud, peaceful, pure.

'That's the star turn, huh. A hundred thousand francs.'

'A hundred thousand,' I whispered. 'Agreed.'

'You're right there, huh,' said Jo, with his hiccoughing laugh.

Then events moved very quickly. There was another explosion very near to us, loud enough to burst our eardrums, but I couldn't say exactly where it had come from. Strangely the roe deer did not move. They just lifted their heads. Then Jo rushed forward, he started to run like a man possessed, he hurtled down the slope whirling his arms round and round, shouting in the direction of the animals to make them move away. One swift movement, a flash and they were gone. Then there was another shot and Jo was hit. He didn't fall immediately, he stayed poised on one leg, you would have said he was about to take flight. It

seemed to last a long time. Then his legs buckled and he
fell. He did not move. I don't know what came over me,
but I found myself flat on my stomach. There was an
incredible silence and yet I could hear every sound: the
wind swaying the pines above my head, the creaking
branches, and everywhere the extraordinary sound of
pine needles like softly falling rain, and my heart thump-
ing against the earth. I raised myself slightly and then
I could see them through the ferns. Three of them stood
near Jo. I don't know where they had come from. They did
not speak or move. Men in hunting gear, with their guns
pointed in front of them. They did not look at Jo. They
looked about them. I was too far away to see their eyes but
I was certain they would discover me, they were looking
around so carefully without moving, as motionless as
statues. My teeth were chattering, I was like a wild animal,
I held my breath. I shoved my face against the ground and
waited. Time passed. Nothing happened. I screwed up my
courage and looked again. They were in the process of
covering Jo very carefully with ferns and branches of
broom. It was happening a long way off, a long way
from me, in a combe, in the middle of a forest, in autumn.

I began slithering backwards, slowly, slowly, using my
knees and elbows. A long time afterwards when I thought
I was far enough off, I raised myself on hands and legs
and started to run, bent double, galloping like a crazed,

terrified animal through bushes, ferns, in any direction at all. I was completely lost, I must have tripped, fallen several times, and I must have vomited. As I ran, I dribbled, I moaned, I took great gulps of air, there was fire in my throat, and I was crying, crying, I wanted my dad to be there to show me the way, and for him not to let me go on like that, running nowhere, for nothing. Once I stopped, my breath was gone, I was at the end of my strength. I thought I saw him. He was standing behind a tree, like when he came to collect me after school. He never dared come to the door. He would stay behind the wall at the end of the street, and then I would run towards him. But he wasn't there, it wasn't possible, and after that I must have reached the road, I'm not sure how, I found myself opposite the petrol station with my car parked on the verge. Nor do I know how I managed to switch on the ignition, but I drove, I drove, at breakneck speed, without a single thought. From time to time I looked in the driving mirror. But in the mirror there was nothing but the empty forest road stretching straight out behind me.

For a long time now I have been telling myself:

'Perhaps it was only a dream after all.'

But once, I couldn't help it, I went that way again. I said to myself:

'At least if I see the shack, the petrol station, perhaps Jo will be in it?' But I didn't find it. I may have taken the wrong road. They all look alike in this forest. I do hope it was all a dream, because soon it will be a year, it's autumn again and nothing's changed. Or rather, since then I have had problems. I left my job and Nad and I have separated. She didn't want to go on. I didn't want to...I can't remember what. And yet it does carry on all the same, *like that*. I need to get away somewhere, but I find it hard to think about it, I need to leave and go somewhere, once and for all, like a stranger.

The Flood

Émile Zola

My name is Louis Roubieu. I am 70 years old, and I was born in the village of Saint-Jory, not far from Toulouse, upstream, on the Garonne. For fourteen years I struggled to make a living from the land. Finally I had enough to live on comfortably and only a month ago I was the richest farmer in the commune.

Our house seemed blessed. Happiness abounded. The sun shone benignly upon us, and I cannot remember a bad harvest. There were nearly a dozen of us on the farm, and we all got on happily together. There was I, still strong and healthy, giving a lead to the children as they worked; my younger brother, Pierre, a bachelor, and formerly a sergeant; then there was my sister Agathe, who had come to live with us after her husband died, an enormous, jolly, masterful woman, whose laugh you could hear from one end of the village to the other. Then came the rest of the brood: my son Jacques, his wife Rose, and their three daughters, Aimée, Véronique, and Marie; the first was married to Cyprien Bouisson, a fine young man with whom she had two little boys, one who was 2 years old, the other, 10 months; the second daughter, only just engaged, who was to marry Gaspard Rabuteau; and lastly, the third, a real young lady, so fair and lilywhite, she looked as if she had been born in a town. That made ten of us. I was a grandfather and a great-grandfather. When we sat down to eat, my sister Agathe was on my right, my brother Pierre on my left. The children were ranged around the table, in order of age, a long line of heads diminishing in size down to the baby of 10 months, already eating his soup like a man. And you should have heard their spoons in the bowls! They were a hungry brood. What jolly talk there was between each mouthful! I felt pride and joy in my veins when the children held out their hands to me and shouted:

'Grandpa, grandpa, give us some bread! . . . A big piece, Grandpa!'

Those were such good times! On our working farm we were happy as the day is long. Pierre invented games in the evenings, regaled us with stories of his regiment. On Sundays Aunt Agathe made cakes for our daughters.

Marie knew hymns by heart and sang them like a little choirgirl. She looked like a saint, with her fair hair tumbling about her neck, and her hands clasped beneath her apron. When Aimée married Cyprien I decided to build on another floor, and I joked that we should have to build another after Véronique wed Gaspard, and if we carried on like that every time someone got married, the house would end up touching the sky. We did not want to leave one another—we would have preferred to build a town on our land behind the farm! When families get on well together it is so good to live and die in your childhood home!

May was magnificent this year. Not for a long time had the harvest shown such promise. And in fact I had gone round the farm that very day with my son Jacques. We had left at about three o'clock. Our fields on the banks of the Garonne stretched out before us in all their young greenness. The grass rose a good three feet and an osier plantation of the previous year already had shoots a yard high. We visited our cornfields and our vines, fields we had bought one by one as we acquired more money. The corn was plentiful, the full-flowering vines promised a superb wine harvest. Jacques gave his hearty laugh and patted me on the shoulder.

'Well, Father, we shan't want for bread or wine again. Is the Almighty a friend of yours, then, that he rains so many riches down on your land?'

We often joked about the poverty we had suffered in the past. Jacques was right, I must have found favour with some saint or God Himself up there in Heaven, for all the good fortune in that land was ours. When it hailed, the hail stopped just at the edge of our fields. If the vines of our neighbours were blighted, there seemed to be a sort of protective wall around ours. And I got to thinking that this was quite right and proper. I didn't do ill to anyone and I thought my good luck was well-deserved.

On the way home we crossed fields that we owned on the other side of the village. The mulberry bushes we had planted were growing beautifully. There were also almond trees that yielded well. We chatted gaily, we made plans. When we had the necessary money we would buy certain plots of land which would join up our property and make us owners of a whole area of the commune. This year's harvest, if it fulfilled its promise, would allow us to realize this dream.

As we got nearer to the house Rose was gesticulating at us and shouting 'Hurry up!'

One of our cows had just calved. Everone was in a high state of excitement about it. Aunt Agathe was massaging the cow's great bulk. The girls were looking at the newborn calf. And the birth of this animal seemed like one more blessing. We had had to have the stables made bigger recently, for now there were almost a hundred head of livestock, mostly cows and sheep, not counting the horses.

'What a wonderful day!' I shouted. 'We'll open some good strong wine and drink to this tonight.'

However, Rose took us on one side and told us that Gaspard, Véronique's fiancé, had come to arrange the wedding day. She had invited him to supper. Gaspard, the eldest son of a farmer from Moranges, was a fine young man of 20, known throughout the region for his prodigious strength. At a fair in Toulouse he had beaten 'Martial, the Lion of the South'. But for all that, he was a gentle fellow with a heart of gold, even a little too shy, and he blushed when Véronique looked directly at him.

I asked Rose to call him in. He was at the back of the yard helping our women who were spreading out the three-monthly wash. When he had come into the dining-room where we all were, Jacques turned to me and said:

'Say something, Father.'

'Well, my boy,' I said, 'have you come to fix the day?'

'Yes, that's right, Père Roubieu,' he answered, with very red cheeks.

'Don't blush, my lad,' I continued. 'If you like, it can be on the feast of Saint Felicity, on the 10th of July. It's now the 23rd of June, so there's not even twenty days to wait.... My poor dead wife was called Felicity, and it will bring you good luck...How does that sound? All right?'

'Yes, let it be the feast of Saint Felicity, Père Roubieu.'

He caught hold of Jacques' hand and mine with a force that would have knocked out a bull. Then he kissed Rose and called her mother. This great lad with the grip of steel loved Véronique to distraction. He told us that he would have been very ill if we had refused him.

'And now,' I went on, 'you'll stay and eat with us?...Come along now, soup all round! Heavens above, I am starving!'

That night eleven of us sat around the table. We had put Gaspard next to Véronique, and he gazed at her incessantly, forgetting to eat, so moved to feel that she belonged to him, that he was sometimes on the brink of tears. Cyprien and Aimée, who had been married for only three years, were smiling. Jacques and Rose, who had already been together for twenty-five years, were rather more serious. And yet their eyes were moist as they secretly exchanged looks, remembering their love in days gone by. As for me, I thought I was coming back to life again when I saw these two lovers, whose happiness made a little corner of paradise at our table. How good the soup tasted that evening! Aunt Agathe, always one for a laugh, risked a few little jokes. Then Pierre began to recount his amorous adventures with a girl from Lyon. Luckily we were having dessert and everyone was talking at once. I had brought two bottles of fortified wine up from the cellar. We drank to the good fortune of Gaspard and Véronique. What we say in our part of the country is: 'good fortune is never to fight, to have lots of children and to amass sackfuls of money.' Then we sang songs. Gaspard knew some love songs in the local dialect. Finally we asked Marie to sing a hymn. She stood up, she had a very delicate, flute-like voice which fell sweetly on our ears.

I had gone over to the window. When Gaspard came over and stood next to me, I said:

'So there's no news from your village?'

'No,' he said. 'They are talking about the heavy rain we've had lately and saying it could well cause some damage.'

In the preceding days it had in fact rained for sixty hours without stopping. The Garonne had been very high since the previous day; but we trusted it, and as long as it didn't rise above the banks we did not consider it a bad neighbour. It served us well! Such a wide, peaceful expanse of water! Besides, we country people don't leave our homes so easily, even when the roof is about to collapse.

'Pah,' I shrugged. 'Nothing will happen. It's the same every year: the river rises and seems to threaten us, as though it is angry, and then it calms down again, innocent as a lamb, the very same night. You will see, my boy. Only fooling, this time too.... Look what lovely weather it is!'

I pointed to the sky. It was seven o'clock and the sun was setting. What a beautiful pure blue sky! The sky was entirely blue, a vast, deep cloak of blue, and in it floated, like a golden cloud, the setting sun. Gradually joy descended from above over the whole horizon. I had never before seen our village settle into such sweet calm. The rosy hue vanished slowly on the roof tiles. I could hear a neighbour laughing, then children's voices on the corner, in front of our farm. Farther off, softened by the distance, the sounds of cattle coming back to their sheds rose to our ears. The Garonne roared continuously. But I was so used to its rumblings that they seemed to me like the sound of silence itself. Gradually the sky became whiter and the village became more somnolent. It was the evening of a beautiful day and it struck me that all our bounteous happiness—the good harvests, our happy home, Véronique's engagement—had come down to us from above in the very purity of that light. A benediction spread among us with the dying of the day.

Meanwhile I had come back into the centre of the room. Our girls were chatting. We were listening to them and smiling, when suddenly, across the hushed tranquillity of the countryside, there rang out a terrible shout, a cry of distress, a cry of death:

'The Garonne, the Garonne!'

We rushed out into the yard.

Saint-Jory lies at the bottom of a dip in the land, lower than the Garonne and roughly five hundred metres away. Curtains of tall poplars dividing the fields completely hide the river.

We could not see anything. But still the cry rang out: 'The Garonne! The Garonne!'

Suddenly two men and three women appeared on the wide path in front of our farm. One of the women was holding a child in her arms. They were the ones who were shouting. They were in panic and running for all they were worth over the hard ground. Sometimes they turned and looked behind them with terrified faces as if a pack of wolves were after them.

'Whatever is wrong?' asked Cyprien. 'Can you see anything, Grandfather?'

'No I can't,' I said. 'There's not a breath of wind.'

In fact, nothing disturbed the low line of the horizon. But just as I was speaking we both let out an exclamation. Behind the people who were running between the trunks of the poplars, in the middle of great tufts of grass, we had just seen something that looked like a pack of wild beasts, grey with yellow spots, advancing towards us. They raised their heads as one, waves crowding upon other waves, in an uncontrollable mass of foaming, fuming white water, making the ground quake as they came on in a silent, mad rush.

It was our turn to let out the same despairing shout:
'The Garonne! The Garonne!'

The two men and three women were still running along the lane. They could hear the terrible galloping waters gaining on them. Now the waves came in one unbroken line, rearing up and collapsing again, with the thunderous noise of a battalion charging. In the first onslaught they had broken down three poplar trees; their tall branches crashed down and disappeared. A wooden hut was overwhelmed; a wall collapsed; unharnessed carts were swept away like straws. But mostly the water seemed to be pursuing those who were fleeing. At the bend in the road, which was very steep at that point, they fell suddenly into an enormous pool and all means of escape were cut off. Yet the people were still running, splashing with great strides through the water, no longer shouting, but crazed and terrified. The water was up to their knees. A huge wave broke over the woman who was carrying the child. Everything was engulfed.

'Quick, quick!' I shouted. 'We have to get inside...The house is solid. We have nothing to fear.'

Prudently we took refuge on the second floor, without delay. We made the women go first. I insisted on going last. The house was built upon a rise above the road. The water invaded the yard gently, not making much noise. We were not particularly alarmed.

'Oh it's nothing,' Jacques said, by way of reassuring the others. 'Do you remember, Father, in '55 the water came up into the yard like that. It was a foot deep. Then it went down again.'

'All the same, it's awful about the harvest,' murmured Cyprien, in a subdued voice.

'No, no. It won't make any difference,' I answered in my turn, seeing the large and pleading eyes of the girls.

Aimée had put her two children in her bed. She stayed at their bedside with Véronique and Marie. Aunt Agathe was talking of warming some wine that she had brought up, to give everyone strength. Jacques and Rose were looking out of the same window. I was in front of the other window with my brother and Cyprien and Gaspard.

'Come on up!' I shouted to the two servant girls, who were paddling around in the middle of the yard. 'Don't stay getting your feet wet.'

'But what about the animals?' they asked. 'They are scared, they will get trampled to death in the stables.'

'No, no, come up . . . We'll see in a little while.'

Saving the livestock was impossible if there was going to be an even worse disaster. I thought it no use scaring everyone, so I made a big show of insouciance. I leaned on the window ledge, chatting and reporting how far the water had risen. The river had made its assault upon the village and now had possession of even the tiniest streets.

The waves were no longer attacking at speed but slowly, and with a deadly sureness, engulfing all. The hollow in which Saint-Jory lies was turning into a lake. In our yard the water was nearly a metre deep. I watched it rise. But I maintained that it was stationary and even went so far as to pretend that it was subsiding.

'So you will have to spend the night here, my boy,' I said, turning to Gaspard, 'unless the roads are clear in an hour or two... which is a possibility.'

He looked at me; his face was very white but he did not speak; and then I saw his eyes on Véronique, full of an inexpressible anguish.

It was half past eight. Outside it was still daylight, but the white light in the pale sky cast a deep sadness over everything. Before the servants came up they had had the foresight to fetch two lamps. I got them lit, thinking that their light would give a little cheer in the room where we had sought refuge, that was already dark. Aunt Agathe, who had moved a table out into the middle of the room, began to organize a card game. That good lady, who from time to time exchanged looks with me, was mainly concerned to keep the children amused. She was splendid in her valiant efforts to remain cheerful, and laughing and joking to combat the fear that she could sense rising all around her. The game started. Aunt Agathe made Aimée, Véronique, and Marie sit round the table. She put the cards in their hands, and played as though she herself too was very involved in the game, shuffling, cutting, dealing the cards and talking nineteen to the dozen so that she almost managed to muffle the sound of the water. But our girls could not be distracted. They remained white-faced, and all ears, fiddling nervously with their hands. The game kept stopping. One of them turned to me and asked in a faint voice:

'Grandfather, is it still rising?'

The water was rising at a frightening rate. I answered in cheery tones:

'No, no, you carry on playing, there is no danger.'

Never had my heart been so tight with anxiety. All the men had placed themselves in front of the windows in order to hide the dreadful spectacle. We tried to smile as we looked towards the interior of the room, at the circle on the table cast by the gentle light of the peaceful evening lamps. It made me think of the winter nights when we were all together around this table. This was the selfsame room, peaceful and filled with warm affection; but while all was calm in front of me, I was listening to the roaring of the unleashed river, rising all the time, at my back.

'Louis,' said my brother Pierre, 'the water is three feet from the window. We must decide what to do.'

I warned him to be quiet, by squeezing his arm. But it was no longer possible to hide the peril. In our stables the animals were drowning. Suddenly there were mooings and bleatings of panicking beasts. And the horses let out those raucous cries that can be heard from such a long way off when they are in mortal danger.

'Oh my God, my God!' Aimée exclaimed. She had stood up, shaking all over, with her hands to her temples.

All the women had risen and we could not stop them rushing to the windows. They stood there silent and transfixed at the hair-raising sight. It was twilight. A sinister clarity floated over the murky expanse of water. The pale sky looked like a white sheet draped over the earth. In the distance were smoky trails, and all was confusion. The day of panic was ending in a night of death. There was no human sound, nothing but the roaring of this ever-widening sea, nothing but the bellowing and neighing of animals!

'My God, my God,' the women said softly, as if they dared not say it aloud.

Their words were cut short by a terrifying crack. The maddened animals had just burst through the stable doors. They were plunged into the yellow water, rolling over and over, carried along by the current. The sheep were swept along like dead leaves, in flocks, swirling round and round. The cows and the horses struggled to find their footing, then lost it again. Above all, our large grey carthorse did not want to die. He reared up, stretched his neck, snorting and blowing like a blacksmith's forge. But the relentless water took him by the crop and we watched as he gave up, beaten.

That was when we started to shout. Despite ourselves, it came up in our throats. We needed to cry aloud. Our hands were held out to all these dear animals who were leaving us, we moaned out loud, without hearing each other, letting out the tears and the sobs we had kept bottled up till then. Oh, it spelled ruin all right! The harvest lost, the livestock drowned, our fortunes changed in the space of a few hours! God was not just. We had done nothing against Him and yet there He was, taking everything away from us. I shook my fist at the horizon. I talked of our walk in the afternoon, the fields, the corn, the vines, that we had believed so full of promise. Was that all a lie then? Happiness was a lie. The sun was a lie, in that it had set with such gentleness and calm in the middle of the great serenity of the evening.

The water continued to rise. Pierre who was watching it shouted to me:

'Louis, we must do something! The water is up to the window!'

This warning dragged us out of our crisis of despair. I came to my senses, saying with a shrug:

'Money is nothing. As long as we are all together, we have nothing to worry about ... Then all we have to do is start work again.'

'Yes, yes, you are right, father,' said Jacques, too quickly. 'And there's no risk, the walls are solid . . . We'll go up on to the roof.'

That was our only refuge now. The water which had been climbing up the stairs step by step with an insistent lapping noise, was already coming in the door. We hurried up to the loft, clutching one another tightly, needing to feel others close, as you do when you are in danger. Cyprien had disappeared. I called to him and saw him coming back from the adjoining rooms, with a distraught expression. Then, as I also noticed that our two servant girls were not there and as I was about to wait for them, he looked at me strangely and said in a low voice:

'Dead. The corner of the shed below their room has just collapsed.'

The poor girls must have been to get their savings from their trunks. He told me, still in a hushed tone, that they had used a ladder which they had placed like a bridge to reach the adjacent building. I warned him to keep quiet about it. A cold breath touched the back of my neck. It was death entering the house.

When it was our turn to go up we didn't even stay to put out the lights. The cards remained spread out on the table. There was already a foot of water in the room.

Luckily the roof was vast and sloped only a little. You reached it by means of a skylight, above which was a sort of platform. It was there that all our family took refuge. The women had sat down. The men were going to try walking on the tiles, as far as the tall chimneys which stood at the two ends of the roof. Leaning against the small window we had climbed through, I scanned the four points of the horizon.

'Help is bound to arrive soon,' I declared stoutly. 'The people in Saintin have boats. They will come past... look there, isn't that a lantern on the water?'

But no one answered. Pierre, without realizing quite what he was doing, had lit his pipe and was smoking so clumsily that he spat out bits of the stem of his pipe with every puff. Jacques and Cyprien looked into the distance with dismal expressions, while Gaspard, clenching his fists, kept walking round the roof as if searching for a way out. At our feet the women huddled together silently, shivering, hiding their faces so as not to see anything; only Rose raised her head, glanced around her and asked:

'What about the servants, where are they? Why aren't they coming up?'

I didn't answer. And then she asked me directly, looking me straight in the eyes:

'So where are the servants?'

I turned away, unable to tell lies to her. And I felt the cold kiss of death, which had already touched me, touch our women and our dear daughters. They had understood. Marie drew herself up to her full height, sighed deeply, then collapsed in a fit of weeping. Aimée kept her two children wrapped in her skirts, hiding them as though to protect them. Véronique, her face in her hands, was very still. Aunt Agathe, also very pale, was making great signs of the cross, and muttering *Paters* and *Aves*.

Yet all around us was a spectacle of sovereign grandeur. Night had really fallen now, but it retained the limpidity of a summer's night. There was no moon, but the star-studded sky was such a pure blue that it looked as if it was filling the air with blue. It still seemed to be dusk, because the horizon remained so clear. And the enormous white pool, widening still beneath the sky, luminous with a clarity of its own, had little flames of phosphorescence which danced on the crest of each wave. You could no longer make out any land, the plain must have been engulfed. I forgot momentarily what danger we were in. One evening, near Marseille, I had seen the sea look like that, and had stood open-mouthed in admiration before it.

'The water is rising, the water is rising,' my brother Pierre repeated. He had allowed his pipe to go out, and continued to break off bits of it in his teeth.

The water was now only a metre from the roof. It no longer had the sleepy look of a tranquil lake. Currents started up in the water. At a certain height we were no longer protected by the ridge of the land before the village. In less than an hour the water became yellow and threatening, rushing at our house, carrying along with it all manner of wreckage, broken barrels, planks of wood, turf. A little way off it was now battering the walls, and we could hear the din of it resounding. Poplars fell with a mortal crack, and houses tumbled down like cartfuls of stones emptied by the side of the road.

Jacques, made desperate by the women's sobbing, kept saying:

'We can't stay here. We must do something. Father, please, please, let us do something.'

I stammered out the words after him:

'Yes, yes, let's do something.'

But we didn't know what. Gaspard offered to take Véronique on his back, to swim off with her. Pierre talked about a raft. It was crazy. Finally Cyprien said:

'If only we could get to the church.'

Above the water the church remained standing, with its small square tower. Seven houses separated us from it. Our farm, which was the first in the village, adjoined a higher building which itself adjoined a neighbour's. Perhaps it would indeed be possible to reach the presbytery by means of the roofs, from where you could easily get into the church. Many people must have taken refuge there already, for the neighbouring roofs were empty and we could hear voices which certainly came from the church tower. But how dangerous it would be to try and get there!

'It's impossible,' said Pierre. 'The Raimbeau's house is too high. We'd need ladders.'

'I'll have a look anyway,' said Cyprien. 'I'll come back if there's no way through. If there is, we'll all go, and carry the girls.'

I let him go. He was right. We had to attempt the impossible. He had just climbed on to the roof of the neighbouring house using an iron clamp that was fixed on to the chimney, when his wife, Aimée, raising her head, saw he was no longer there. She shouted:

'Where is he? I don't want him to leave me. We live together, we shall die together.'

When she saw him on top of the house she ran out onto the tiles, still clutching her children, shouting: 'Cyprien, wait for me. I'm coming too, I want to die with you.'

She kept walking. He leaned down and begged her to go back, insisting that he would return, that he was doing it for the safety of everyone. But half-crazed, she shook her head, repeating:

'I'm coming with you, I'm coming with you.'

He had to take the children. Then he helped her to climb up. We were able to follow their progress along the ridge of the house. They were walking slowly. She had taken her weeping children back into her arms, and he, at every step, turned to support her.

'Get her to safety and come back straight away!' I cried.

I saw him wave his hand, but the roaring of the water prevented me from hearing his reply. Soon we couldn't see them any more. They had climbed down on to the other house which was lower than the first. Five minutes later they reappeared on the third, whose roof must have been very steep, for they were making their way slowly along the top of it on hands and knees. Suddenly I was seized with panic. I cupped my fingers and started to shout with all my might:

'Come back! Come back!'

All of us, Pierre, Jacques, and Gaspard, were shouting to them to come back. Our voices made them stop momentarily. But then they went on again. Now they were at the angle formed by the road, opposite the Raimbeau's house, a tall building whose roof was at least three metres higher than the neighbouring houses. They hesitated for an instant. Then Cyprien, with the agility of a cat, climbed around the flue of one of the chimneys. Aimée, who must have agreed to wait for him, remained standing in the middle of the tiles. We could make her out quite clearly, clutching her children to her chest, black and seeming bigger against the clear sky. And that's when the terrible catastrophe began.

The Raimbeau's house, at first intended for industrial use, was not very solidly built. Moreover, its front bore the full impact of the currents of water in the street. I thought I saw it shake beneath the onslaught. And with my throat constricting, I watched Cyprien crossing the roof. Suddenly we heard a roaring noise. The moon was rising freely in the sky, a round moon with a yellow face lighting up the immense lake as brightly as a lamp. Not one detail of the disaster was lost to us. It was the Raimbeau's house that had just gone down. We uttered cries of terror when we watched Cyprien disappear. Of the collapse all we could see was the water in turmoil, and waves splashing up again under the debris of the roof. Then it was calm once more; the vast lake found its level again around the black cavity of the drowned house with its carcase of broken planks sticking up out of the water. There was a mass of tangled beams, a wooden framework as big as a cathedral, half destroyed. And in among those beams I imagined I could see a body moving, something living that was making a last superhuman effort.

'He's alive!' I shouted. 'Oh, God be praised, he's alive!... There, above that white pool of moonlight!'

We were shaken by a nervous laughter. We were clapping for joy, as though we ourselves were saved.

'He'll come up again,' said Pierre.

'Yes, yes, look,' said Gaspard, 'look, there he is, he's trying to catch hold of that beam on the left!'

But then we stopped laughing. Not another word was said, anxiety seized our throats. We had just realized how dire Cyprien's situation was. When the house collapsed, his feet were trapped in between two beams. And he remained hanging there, head down, unable to free himself, a few centimetres from the water. It was an appalling agony. On the roof of the neighbouring house, Aimée stood with the two children, shaking convulsively. She was witnessing the death of her poor husband a few feet below, and she did not for a single second avert her gaze from him. She kept up a continuous screaming, like the howling of a dog maddened by the horror.

'We can't let him die like that,' said Jacques, frantic. 'We must go to him.'

'Perhaps we could get down among the beams,' Pierre said. 'We might be able to free him.'

They were making their way to the neighbouring rooftops when the second house collapsed too. Their route was cut off. Then the cold entered into us. Automatically we had caught hold of each other's hands. We squeezed them so hard it hurt, all the while unable to take our eyes off the horrendous spectacle.

Cyprien at first had attempted to straighten himself. With an extraordinary strength he managed to pull himself clear of the water and keep his body in a slant position. But fatigue was getting the better of him. He still struggled, trying to catch hold of the beams, flailed around with his arms to see if there was something he could cling to. Then, accepting death, he fell back, once more hanging, losing the fight. Death was a long time coming. His hair was scarcely in the water, which was rising, slowly but surely. He must have felt the coolness on the top of his head. A first wave dampened his forehead. Others came and closed his eyes. Slowly, as we watched, his head disappeared.

The women, at our feet, had buried their faces in their hands. We too fell to our knees, our arms outstretched, weeping, babbling our prayers. On the roof Aimée was still standing with her children clasped against her, and howling louder and louder into the night.

I don't know how long we remained stupefied by this tragedy. When I came to my senses, the water had risen even more. Now it was reaching the tiles. The roof was nothing more than a narrow island emerging from the

huge lake. To right and left the houses must have collapsed. A sea stretched out around us.

'We're moving,' murmured Rose, clinging to the tiles.

And indeed we all had the sensation of rolling, as
though the roof had been swept away and had become a
raft. It seemed we were being carried along by the great tide
of water. Then, when we looked at the church tower opposite, still there, unmoving, our vertigo ceased. We were
back again in the same place in the heavy swell of the waves.

Then the water began its assault. Till now the current
had followed the course of the road. But the detritus that
was in its way now made it change direction. It was a well-
regulated attack. As soon as some flotsam, a beam perhaps, got within reach of the current, it took it, balanced
it, then flung it against the house like a battering-ram.
And it did not let go, but dragged it back, to fling it
forward again, a redoubling of blows, time after time,
against our walls. Soon ten or twelve beams came battering at us from all sides simultaneously. The water roared.
Foam spattered on to our feet. We could hear the sound of
a faint groaning from inside the house full of water, whose
walls were already cracking. Whenever the attacks were
particularly violent and the beams in the water were
hitting us full on we thought the end had come and that
the walls were opening and delivering us up to the river
through their gaping cracks.

Gaspard, the wrestler, had ventured out to the very edge of the roof. He managed to reach a beam and heave it up in his strong arms.

'We have to defend ourselves,' he shouted.

Jacques, for his part, was trying to catch hold of a long pole as it went by. Pierre helped him. I cursed my age, which left me without any strength, as weak as a child. But we were organizing our defences. It was a duel, three men against a river. Gaspard held his beam at the ready, waiting for the planks of wood that the strong current had made into battering rams. And he stopped them forcibly at a short distance from the walls. Sometimes the blow was so violent that he would fall. Next to him Jacques and Pierre were manoeuvring the long pole, also keeping back the debris. For nearly an hour the useless struggle continued. They gradually lost their reason, swearing, dealing blows at the water, throwing insults at it. Gaspard was slashing around as though in one-to-one combat, using the end of his piece of wood as though he were driving it into someone's chest. And the water remained, calmly obstinate, unharmed and invincible. Then Jacques and Pierre on the roof gave up the struggle, exhausted. Gaspard with one last effort allowed his plank of wood to be taken by the current and it pounded at us. All resistance was impossible.

Marie and Véronique had thrown themselves into each other's arms. They uttered, in broken voices over and over again, words that still echo in my ears:

'I don't want to die! . . . I don't want to die!'

Rose had her arms around them. She was trying to console and comfort them. But she herself, trembling, lifted up her face and shouted despite herself:

'I don't want to die!'

Only Aunt Agathe said nothing. She was no longer praying, no longer crossing herself. She looked around, dazed, making an effort to smile when she met my eyes.

The water was now beating against the tiles. We had no hope of help. We could still hear voices from the direction of the church. At one point two lanterns had passed by in the distance. But the silence fell once more and the yellow lake spread itself in all its naked immensity. The people of Saintin who had boats must have been taken by surprise before we were.

Gaspard, however, went on prowling around the roof. Suddenly he called to us. And he said:

'Come here! . . . Help me. Hold on tight to me.'

He had taken hold of the pole again. He was waiting for an enormous piece of debris, which was floating gently towards the house. It was a large piece of shed roof made out of solid planks which the water had snatched in one piece and which was floating like a raft. When this piece of roof came within his grasp he caught it with his pole. And as he felt himself being pulled away, he shouted to us for help. We had seized hold of him by the waist and we held on tight. Then, as soon as the wreckage entered the current, it came on all by itself, crashing against our roof with such force that for a minute we feared to see it break into little pieces.

Boldly, Gaspard jumped on to this raft that chance had sent our way. He walked to and fro on it, testing how solid it might be, while Pierre and Jacques hung on to it against the edge of the roof. And he laughed happily, saying:

'Grandfather, we are saved... Girls, stop crying!... A real boat. Look, my feet are dry. And it will easily carry us all. We shall be quite at home on this!'

However, he thought it necessary to strengthen it. He seized hold of the planks that were floating around, tied them with the ropes that luckily Pierre had brought with him when we left the bedrooms below. He even fell into the water, but when we cried out he laughed even more. The water was his friend, he could swim for miles along the Garonne. Once more up on the raft he shook himself, shouting: 'Come on now, get on board, let's not waste time.'

The women were on their knees. Gaspard had to carry Véronique and Marie to the middle of the raft, where he made them sit down. Rose and Aunt Agathe slithered down the tiles by themselves and went to sit by the girls. At that moment I glanced in the direction of the church. Aimée was still there. She had her back to a chimney now and was holding the children up in the air at arm's length, for the water was already up to her waist.

'Don't worry, grandfather,' Gaspard said to me. 'We will pick her up as we go past, I promise.'

Pierre and Jacques had climbed on to the raft. I jumped on as well. It was leaning a bit to one side but it really was solid enough to carry us all. Gaspard left the roof last of all, telling us to take some poles he had gathered and which were to be our oars. He himself had a very long pole and was using it with great dexterity. We took our orders from him. At his command we all pressed our poles against the tiles to push off, but it seemed as if the raft was glued to the roof. In spite of all our efforts we could not get it away. At each new attempt the current smashed us back against the house. And that was the most dangerous manoeuvre, for every time it happened the crash threatened to smash the planks on which we were standing.

And so again we felt our own impotence. We had believed that we were saved and yet we were still the creatures of the river. I even regretted that the women were no longer on the roof. For every minute I could imagine them being thrown off and sucked into the furious current. But when I spoke of getting back to our place of safety, they all shouted:

'No. No, let's try again. Better to die here!'

Gaspard was no longer laughing. We renewed our efforts, leaning on the poles with redoubled energy. Pierre finally had the idea of going back on to the tiled roof and dragging us to the left with the help of a rope. In this way he could perhaps lead us away from the current. Then, once he had jumped back on to the raft, with a few strokes of the pole we would be free. But Gaspard remembered the promise he had given me to go and collect our poor Aimée, who had not ceased her plaintive howling. To do that, we had to cross the road, where this terrible current, which we had just been fighting, was as strong as ever. He looked questioningly at me. I was at my wits' end. Never had I been faced with such a choice. We were going to put eight lives at risk. And yet, though I hesitated for a moment, I did not have the strength to reject this dire appeal.

'Yes, yes,' I said to Gaspard. 'It's impossible, we can't go without her.'

He lowered his head without a word and with his pole began to push it against all the walls still standing. We were floating along the side of the neighbours' house, above our stables. But as soon as we came out on to the street, we cried out. The current took us again and was carrying us off back to our own house. For some seconds

we were in a giddy spin, borne along like a leaf, so rapidly
that our shouts ended in the terrible blow of the raft
against the tiles. There was a cracking sound, the planks
came apart and spun round and round, and we were all
thrown into the water. I don't know what happened then.
I remember that as I fell I saw Aunt Agathe held up by her
skirts, spread out on the water. She was sinking, without a
struggle.

A sharp pain made me open my eyes. It was Pierre
pulling me by the hair along the tiles. I lay there looking,
only half-conscious of what was going on. Pierre had just
dived in again. And in my dazed state I was surprised to
see Gaspard all of a sudden, in the place where my brother
had vanished. The young man was carrying Véronique in
his arms. When he had put her next to me, he threw
himself back in again, drew out Marie, whose face was
waxen, stiff and immobile, so I thought she was dead.
Then he jumped in again. But this time he searched in
vain. Pierre had joined him. Both were speaking and
giving each other directions that I could not hear. As
they were getting back on to the roof, exhausted, I cried:

'What about Aunt Agathe? And Jacques and Rose?'

They shook their heads. Huge tears poured from their
eyes. By the few words they uttered I gathered that
Jacques' head had been battered by a plank. Rose had
clung to the body of her husband and it had carried her

away. Aunt Agathe had not reappeared. We assumed that her body, pulled by the current, had gone back into our house below us through an open window.

I lifted myself and looked towards the roof to which Aimée had been clinging only a few minutes before. But the water was still rising. Aimée was no longer howling. I saw two arms held up straight to keep her children out of the water. Then they were swallowed up, the watery expanse closed over them in the sleeping moonlight.

There were only five of us left on the roof. The water left us not much more than a narrow band along the ridge. One of the chimneys had just been swept away. We had to lift Véronique and Marie, who had passed out, and hold them almost upright, so that the waves would not wet their legs. Finally they regained consciousness and our worries increased when we saw they were soaked and shivering, and crying again that they did not want to die. We reassured them, as you reassure children, telling them that they were not going to die, that we would make certain of that. But they no longer believed us, they knew very well that they were going to die. And each time the word 'die' sounded like a knell, their teeth started chattering, their terror made them fall upon each others' necks.

The end had come. Around us nothing could be seen in our broken village but a few pieces of wall. Only the church held its tower intact, and from there voices still came, a murmuring from people sheltering. In the distance the enormous flood was roaring. We could not even hear the houses collapsing any more, like carts suddenly tipping stones. All was abandonment, a shipwreck in the middle of the ocean, a thousand miles from land.

At one moment we thought we could detect on our left the sound of rowing. You would have said it was the soft thud of oars, rhythmic, getting clearer and clearer. What sweet music to our ears! We all sat up straight, one question in our minds. We held our breath, but we could see nothing. The yellow expanse of water, stained with black shadows, stretched out before us, but not one of those shadows, the tops of trees, the remains of broken walls, was moving. Bits of flotsam, grass, empty barrels, deceived us into a false delight. We waved our handkerchiefs until, realizing our mistake, we fell back into despair because of the noise that we kept hearing, without us being able to discover where it was coming from.

'Ah, I can see it,' cried Gaspard suddenly. 'Look, over there! A big boat!'

And, his arm outstretched, he pointed to a dot in the distance. I could see nothing, nor could Pierre. But Gaspard insisted. It really was a boat. The noise of oars could be heard more distinctly. So at last we saw it too. It was moving slowly, and looked to be going round us but not getting any nearer. I remember that at that moment we were like madmen. We raised our arms in a fury, uttered cries loud enough to hurt our throats. And we hurled insults at the boat, calling it cowardly. Still black and silent, it sailed around us more slowly. Was it really a boat? I still don't know. When we saw it disappear, as we thought, it bore away with it our last hope.

From then on, every second, we were expecting to be swallowed up by the house falling. It was badly undermined, no doubt held up solely by some large wall and would be swept away in its entirety when that collapsed. But what I feared most was feeling the roof give way under our weight. The house would have perhaps held all night long, but the tiles were weakening, because of the battering and the holes made by the beams. We had taken refuge on the left side, on rafters that were still intact. But then these very rafters seemed to weaken. They would certainly give way if all five of us remained huddled in such a small space.

Some minutes ago, my brother Pierre had put his pipe back in his mouth, with a mechanical gesture. He was twisting his old military moustache and frowning, muttering words that were indistinct. The growing danger that surrounded him and against which his courage was useless had begun to try his patience unbearably. He spat three or four times into the water in anger and disgust.

Then as we were still sinking, he made up his mind and climbed down the roof.

'Pierre, Pierre,' I cried in alarm, realizing what he was doing.

'Adieu, Louis...I'm afraid it's too long-drawn-out for me. It will make more room for you.'

And having first thrown in his pipe, he jumped in himself, adding:

'Goodnight, I've had enough.'

He did not come up again. He was a mediocre swimmer. He no doubt abandoned himself to the waves, his heart broken by our disaster and the death of all our family, not wishing to survive them.

The church bell chimed two. The night was coming to an end, this dreadful night that was already so full of agony and tears. Gradually beneath our feet the dry space was shrinking. There was the murmur of running water, little waves that caressed and played and pushed, one after the other. The current had changed again. The flotsam was travelling to the right of the village, floating slowly as if the waters, about to reach their highest level, were weary and indolent and had reached a resting point.

Suddenly Gaspard pulled off his shoes and his jacket. I had seen him clasping his hands and bruising his fingers for some little while. And when I questioned him, he said:

'Listen grandfather, I shall die if I stay here. I can't wait any longer... Let me go, I'll save her.'

He was talking about Véronique. I wanted to argue. He would never have the strength to carry the young woman into the church. But he insisted.

'I'll be all right, I've got good arms and I'm strong... You'll see!' He added that he preferred to attempt the rescue straight away, that he was starting to feel as weak as a child when he heard the house crumble away like that beneath our feet.

'I love her, I'll save her,' he repeated.

I remained silent, pulling Marie to my chest. So he thought I was blaming him for thinking solely of his beloved, and stammered:

'I'll come back for Marie I swear. I'll find a boat and organize some kind of rescue... Trust me grandfather.'

He kept his trousers on, nothing else. And in a low voice rapidly he gave Véronique his orders. She was not to struggle, she was to let herself go freely, she was above all not to be scared. At each phrase the young girl said yes, distractedly. Finally, after having made the sign of the cross, although he wasn't at all religious normally, he allowed himself to slide down the roof holding Véronique by a rope that he had tied under her arms. She uttered a loud cry, beat at the water with her arms and legs, then could not breathe, and she fainted.

'That's better for me,' Gaspard shouted. 'Now I can take charge of her.'

You can imagine how anxiously I watched them go. On the white water I could make out Gaspard's every movement. He was holding the girl up with the help of the rope that he had tied around his own neck. And he was carrying her like that, half thrown across his right shoulder. The crushing weight pulled him down from time to time. But he was making some progress, as he swam with superhuman strength. I was no longer in doubt, and he had covered a third of the distance already, when he crashed into some hidden wall in the water. The blow was terrible. Both of them disappeared. Then I saw him reappear alone. The rope must have broken. He dived down twice. Finally he came up again, bringing Véronique on to his back. But he no longer had a rope to hold her and she was pulling him down more. However, he was still making progress. I was overcome by trembling as he got nearer and nearer the church. Suddenly I wanted to shout out as I saw some planks coming at them from the side. My mouth remained wide open. A new blow had separated them and the waters closed over them.

From that moment on I was in a dazed state. All I had was an animal instinct for self-preservation. When the water advanced, I retreated. In this stupor I could hear someone laughing but I had no explanation as to who could be laughing like that next to me. It was daybreak, a great white dawn. It was pleasantly cool and very quiet, like on the edge of a lake whose waters are stirring before sunrise. But the laughter was still ringing in my ears, and when I turned, I found Marie standing in her wet clothes. She was laughing.

The poor dear creature, how sweet, how pretty she was at that hour of the morning! I saw her lean down and take some water in the hollow of her hand and wash her face. Then she twisted up her beautiful blond hair and knotted it behind her head. There was no doubt she was getting washed and ready, believing she was in her little bedroom on Sunday when the bells rang out gaily. And she carried on laughing her childlike laugh, her eyes clear and her face happy.

As for me I started to laugh too, infected with her madness. Terror had made her mad and it was a blessing from heaven, she seemed so delighted with the pure spring morning.

I let her hasten, uncomprehending, nodding her head sweetly. She was still making herself pretty. Then, when she thought she was ready to go, she sang one of her hymns in her fine crystalline voice. But soon she left off and shouted as though responding to a voice which was calling her and which she alone could hear:

'I'm coming! I'm coming!'

She started singing hymns again, went down the roof and entered the water, which covered her gently without causing her distress. I had not stopped smiling. I looked contentedly at the place where she had just disappeared.

After that I remember nothing. I was alone on the roof. The water had risen further. One chimney remained standing, and I think I was clinging on to it with all my strength, like an animal that does not want to die. After that nothing, nothing, a black hole, just nothingness.

Why am I still here? They say the people from Saintin came about six o'clock with boats and found me lying on a chimney pot, unconscious. The waters were so cruel as not to carry me off while I could not feel my misfortune, after they had taken all my family.

I, an old man, am the one who has insisted on staying alive. All the rest have gone, the babes in arms, the young women ready for marriage, the young couples, the older couples. And here am I still alive, dried out and useless, a weed rooted amongst the stones! If I had the courage I would do the same as Pierre and say: 'I've had enough. Goodnight!' And I should throw myself into the Garonne and take the road all the others have taken. I have no children, my house is in ruins, my fields are destroyed. In the evenings when we were at supper, all of us, the old ones in the middle, the young ones in order around the table, I was surrounded and warmed by their laughter! Oh those great days of the hay and wine harvest when we were all at work and we came home full of pride in our riches! The lovely children, lovely vines, the lovely girls and the lovely corn, the joy of my old age and the living reward of my whole life! Since all that is gone, my God, why should I live?

There is no consolation. I don't want any help. I shall give my land to the people of the village who still have children. They will find the strength to get rid of all the wreckage and cultivate the land again. When you have lost all your children you only need a small plot to die in.

I have only one desire, one last one. I should have liked to find the bodies of my loved ones, so that I could bury them in our cemetery under a stone, where I could have gone to be with them. They were saying that they had fished up a whole lot of bodies in Toulouse that had been carried off in the river. I have decided to try and go there.

What a terrible catastrophe! Nearly two thousand houses in ruins! Seven hundred deaths. All the bridges swept away. The whole area destroyed, drowned in mud. Frightful tragedies. Twenty thousand poor people half naked and dying of hunger. The town poisoned with corpses, terrified by the possibility of typhoid. Mourning everywhere, the roads full of funeral cortèges and dona- tions of alms insufficient to dress the wounds. But I walked in the midst of these ruins, my eyes seeing nothing. I had my own ruins, my own dead, and they crushed me utterly.

I was told that many bodies had indeed been recovered. They had already been buried in long lines in a corner of the cemetery. But people had taken care to photograph the ones not from the town. And it was amongst these pathetic portraits that I found those of Gaspard and Véronique. The two fiancés had stayed bound to one another in death, exchanging their wedding kiss in a passionate embrace. They were still holding on to each other so hard with their arms outstretched and the mouths joined that you would have had to break their limbs to separate them. That is how they were photographed together and were sleeping together beneath the earth.

That is all I have—that terrible image of them, those two lovely young people swollen by the water, disfigured, their livid faces still retaining the heroism of their love. I look at them and I weep.

CUISS...
TRADITIONNELLE

LA NATURE

PAIN AU
LEVAIN

FARINES A LA
MEULE DE PIERRE

The Beaucaire Coach

Alphonse Daudet

It was the day I arrived. I had taken the Beaucaire coach, a good old bone-shaker that does not have to cover a great distance before it gets back again but dawdles, so it appears to have come from a very long way away. There were five of us on top not counting the driver.

First, a cattle man from the Camargue, a small, thick-set chap, hairy and malodorous, with large bloodshot eyes and silver rings in his ears; then two people from Beaucaire, a baker and his son-in-law, both very red and wheezy, but with superb profiles, like two Roman coins of Vitellius. Lastly, sitting at the front, near the driver, a

298 ■ Alphonse Daudet

man...no! a *cap*, an enormous rabbit-skin cap, which
hardly spoke at all and contemplated the road ahead
with a sad expression.

All those people knew one another and talked aloud
about their doings, quite freely. The Camargue man was
saying that he came from Nîmes, having been summoned
by the magistrate for having prodded a shepherd with a
fork. They are a hot-blooded lot in the Camargue...And
in Beaucaire too, come to that! Believe it or not, our
two men from Beaucaire wanted to cut one another's
throats on account of the Holy Virgin. It seems that the
baker came from a parish which had long been dedicated
to the Madonna, the one the Provençals call the *good
mother*, holding the infant Jesus in her arms; the son-in-
law, on the other hand, sang in the choir of a modern
church dedicated to the Immaculate Conception, that
beautiful smiling image with her arms by her side and
her hands full of rays of light. That was the reason for
their quarrel. You should have seen how those two good
Catholics behaved to one another, they and their madonnas:

'A fine woman, your *Immaculate Virgin!*'

'Don't talk to me about your *good mother!*'

'She saw a thing or two in Palestine, your madonna!'

'What about yours, ugly old thing! Who knows what
she got up to...Just ask Saint Joseph.'

You might have thought you were in the port in Naples, all it wanted was the flash of knives, and I truly believe this fine theological contest would have ended thus if the driver had not intervened.

'Enough of your madonnas,' he laughed to the two from Beaucaire. 'That's all women's stuff. Men shouldn't have anything to do with it.'

Whereupon he cracked his whip in a gesture of scepticism that brought everyone into line with his way of thinking.

The argument ceased; but the baker, having got going, was determined to deliver himself of the rest of his witty remarks, and, turning to the unfortunate rabbit-cap, silent and sad in his corner, he said mockingly:

'And what about your wife then, grinder? . . . Which parish does she support?'

There must have been a hugely comical intention in this sentence, for the whole of the top of the coach erupted in noisy laughter . . . The grinder wasn't laughing, though. He was pretending not to hear. Seeing that, the baker turned to me:

'Don't you know his wife, monsieur? She's *some* parishioner! Nobody in Beaucaire to touch her.'

The laughter increased. The grinder did not move; without raising his head, he simply muttered:

'Shut up, baker.'

But the devilish baker would not be quiet. He went on even more:

'Lucky man with a wife like that, by God. You wouldn't be bored for a moment with her... Just think! A lovely woman who allows herself to be seduced every six months, she's always got something new to tell you about when she comes home... Yes, it's a strange marriage... Imagine that, monsieur, they hadn't been married twelve months when off she goes to Spain with a chap who sells chocolate.

'Her husband stays at home weeping and drinking... It drove him mad. After some time the lady comes back home, dressed in Spanish style, with little castanets. We all said to her:

"Keep out of his way, he'll kill you."

'Well, as for killing her... they calmly got back together again and she taught him to play the Basque castanets.'

There was another explosion of laughter. In his corner, without raising his head, the grinder muttered again:

'Shut up, baker.'

The baker took no notice, but continued:

'Perhaps you are thinking, monsieur, that when she got back from Spain the woman behaved herself... Oh no ... Her husband had taken it so well! It made her feel like doing it again ... After the Spaniard, it was an officer, then a sailor on the Rhône, then a musician, then a ... Who else? The best of it was that each time it was the same pantomime. The wife goes off, the husband weeps; she comes back, he is consoled. And she gets seduced all the time and he always takes her back ... You have to admit he's very patient, her husband! I must say too that she's a stunner, the grinder's little wife ... Fit for a cardinal: lively, attractive, nice figure, soft white skin, and hazel eyes that look at men with a twinkle in them ... My word, Parisian, if you are ever passing through Beaucaire again ...'

'Oh for God's sake shut up ...' said the poor grinder once more in a broken voice.

At that moment the coach halted. We were at the *mas* des Anglores. It was there the two men from Beaucaire got out, and I swear I didn't try to stop them ... What a joker, that baker! You could still hear him laughing, even in the yard.

Once that lot had gone, the top of the coach seemed empty. We had dropped the man from the Camargue in Arles; the driver was walking along the road beside his horses ... We were alone on top, the grinder and myself, each in his corner, not talking. It was hot; the leather hood of the coach was burning. From time to time I felt my eyes close and my head get heavier, but it was impossible to sleep. The words 'Shut up, for God's sake,' so upsetting and so softly spoken, still sounded in my ears...He couldn't sleep either, the poor man! From behind I saw his large shoulders shaking and his hand—a long, pallid, stupid hand—trembling on the back of the seat, like an old man's. He was weeping...

'Here you are, Parisian, home!' the driver suddenly shouted; and pointing with his whip he showed me my green hill with the windmill stuck on the top like a large butterfly.

I made haste to get down...As I passed next to the grinder, I tried to look under his cap! I should have liked to see him before I left. As if understanding me, the unfortunate man suddenly raised his head and fixing his eyes on mine said dully:

'Have a good look at me, my friend, and if one day something bad happens in Beaucaire, you can say you know the man who did it.'

He had a sad, lifeless face, with little faded eyes. There were tears in them, but in his voice there was hatred. Hatred is the anger of the weak!...If I were the grinder's wife, I should watch out...

The Pope's Mule

Alphonse Daudet

Of all the picturesque sayings, saws, or proverbs with
which our locals in Provence lace their everyday speech,
I know of none more quaint or peculiar than this. Fifteen
leagues around my windmill, when they talk about a man
who is spiteful or vindictive they say: 'Beware of that
man! He is like the pope's mule, he holds his kick for
seven years.'

For a very long time now I have tried to find out where
this saying could have come from. What was this papal
mule and the kick that he held for seven years? Nobody
here could enlighten me, not even Francet Mamaï, the
fife-player, though he knows his Provençal legends like the
back of his hand. Francet thinks, as I do, that it must be

some old tale from the area round Avignon, but he has never heard of it except in the proverb.

'Try the Bibliothèque des Cigales,' said the old fife-player, with a laugh. 'That's the only place you might find out.'

This seemed a good idea, and as the Bibliothèque des Cigales is on my doorstep, I went and shut myself up in there for a week.

The library is magnificent, the fixtures admirable, open for poets night and day and staffed by little librarians with percussive instruments who make music for you all the while. I spent some delightful days in there and after a week of research—on my back—I finally found what I was looking for, the story of my mule and the famous kick that he held back for seven years. It is a pleasant, if rather simple, little tale, and I shall try to tell it just as I read it yesterday morning in a manuscript the colour of time, which smelled of dried lavender and was marked by threads of gossamer.

He who has not seen Avignon at the time of the popes has seen nothing. Never was there a town like it for jollity, bustle, animation, for festivals taking place one after another. From morn till night there were processions, pilgrimages, roads strewn with flowers and magnificently draped, cardinals arriving on the Rhône, banners floating in the wind and ships decked out with bunting, the pope's soldiers chanting Latin in the squares, monks rattling their begging bowls. Houses and workplaces crowded one on top of the other around the grand papal palace and buzzed like bees around the hive with the clatter of lace-makers, the to-and-fro of their shuttles weaving the golden chasubles, the little hammers of the *burette* makers, the tuning of the instrument makers, the singing of the women weaving. And over all this was the sound of the bells, and always, down by the bridge, a beating of *tambourins*. For in this part of the world when people are happy they must dance, they must dance; and as at that time the streets were too narrow for the farandole, they took their fifes and *tambourins* on to the bridge of Avignon, in the fresh air of the Rhône, and night and day they danced, they danced ... Oh, what a blessed time, what a blessed town! Halberds never used in anger; state prisons in which the wine was placed to cool. Never any shortages, never any war ... That's how good the Comtat popes were at governing; that's why their people were so sorry when they went.

One in particular, a nice old man called Boniface ... When he died there was many a tear shed in Avignon! He was such a kind, such a gracious prince. He smiled at you so benevolently from astride his mule. And when you passed by near to him, whether you were an insignificant producer of madder or the Magistrate himself he gave you his blessing in the most courteous manner. He was a real Yvetot pope, but a Provençal one; there was something rather subtle about the way he laughed, a stalk of marjoram in his lapel and not the slightest sign of a 'Jeanneton'. The only Jeanneton this good priest was ever known to have had was his vineyard—a small vineyard he had planted himself, three leagues outside Avignon in the country of Château-Neuf where the myrtles grow.

Every Sunday after Vespers this worthy man would go and pay court to his vineyard, and when he was up there, sitting in the warm sunshine with his mule by his side, his cardinals stretched out around him under the vines, he would uncork a flask of vintage wine—the beautiful ruby wine that ever since has been called Chateauneuf du Pape—and sip it delicately, looking fondly at his vines the while. Then once the flask was empty and the sun was setting he would return, quite content, to the town, with all his entourage. And when he crossed the bridge in Avignon, in the midst of the drums and farandoles his mule, spurred on by the music, broke into a little ambling trot, while he himself kept time to the dance with his *biretta*, which scandalized the cardinals but made everyone else remark: 'What a good prince! What a worthy pope!'

What the pope loved most of all next to his vineyard in Château-Neuf was his mule. The old man was crazy about that animal. Every evening before he went to bed, he went to check that her stable was safely locked, and see if she needed anything in her manger, and he would never leave the table until, under his supervision, a big bowl of wine had been prepared *à la française*, with plenty of sugar and herbs, which he took her himself, in spite of the remarks made by the cardinals. I ought to state here that the animal really was worth it. She was a beautiful black mule, with reddish markings, sure-footed, with a glossy coat and a wide, substantial rump; she carried her neat little head with pride, all decked out with pompoms, bows, silver bells, and ribbons. She had an angelic nature as well, a candid gaze, and two long ears that kept flicking back and forth and gave her an air of innocence. The whole of Avignon treated her with respect, and when she was out in the town she received all manner of courtesies; for everyone knew this was the best way to gain favour in the court, and that, with her innocent air, the pope's mule had made the fortunes of more than one man, of which Tistet Védène and his astonishing adventure was the proof.

This Tistet Védène was, in fact, a thoroughgoing rascal. His father, Guy Védène, the goldsmith, had been forced to throw him out because he was idle and was setting a bad example to the apprentices. For six months he could be seen trailing through all the gutters of Avignon, but mainly in the area of the papal palace. For this young man had for a long time entertained an idea about the pope's mule, and, as you will see, it was rather a clever one... One day when His Holiness was walking all alone under the ramparts with his animal, young Tistet accosted him and said, clasping his hands in admiration:

'Good gracious, Holy Father, what a noble mule you have there!... Let me have a little look at her... Oh, what a fine mule, sir!... The Emperor of Germany himself does not have one to equal yours.'

And he stroked her and spoke to her gently as if to a young girl. 'Come now, my jewel, my treasure, my precious pearl...'

And the good pope, much moved, thought to himself: 'What a fine young man!... How kind he is to my mule!'

And then do you know what happened the very next day? Tistet Védène exchanged his old yellow jacket for a handsome lace alb, a cape of purple silk and shoes with buckles, and entered the service of the pope, where never before had any save for noblemen's sons and cardinals' nephews been received... There's intrigue for you!... But Tistet did not stop at that.

Once in the service of the pope, the rogue carried on playing the tricks which had brought him such success. Though insolent with everybody else, he was attentive and considerate to the mule, and you were always meeting him in the palace courtyards with his hands full of oats or sainfoin, gently shaking the rose-coloured bunches, and looking up at the Holy Father's balcony, as much as to say: 'Who do you think these are for, then?' So much so that in the end the good pope, who felt he was getting old, reached the stage where he left it to him to keep watch on the stable and to take the mule her bowl of wine *à la française*. The cardinals were not amused.

The mule was not amused either... For now, at the time for her to have her wine, five or six little clerics arrived and hid in the straw with their gowns and their lace. Then after a moment or two a lovely scent of caramel and herbs filled the stable and Tistet Védène would appear, carefully bearing the bowl of wine *à la française*. And then the poor animal's torments would begin.

This aromatic wine which she loved so much, which warmed her and put the spring in her step, they were so cruel as to take it to her there in her stall and let her have a whiff of it. Then as soon as it filled her nostrils, in a trice it was gone! The entire beautiful, flame-coloured liquor disappeared down the throats of those rascals... And if only all they had done was steal her wine! But they were like devils when they had had something to drink, all those little clerics!... One of them would pull her ears, the other her tail. Quiquet got on her back, Beluguet tried his *biretta* on her, and it did not cross any of these rascals' minds that with one kick of her hind legs the noble beast could have sent them all flying to the Pole Star or further still. But no! Not for nothing was she the pope's mule, the mule of blessings and indulgences... The children might do their worst, she did not get angry. It was only against Tistet Védène that she bore a grudge. When she sensed Tistet behind her, she felt her hooves itching—and truly she had good reason. The good-for-nothing Tistet played such dirty tricks on her! He dreamed up such cruel pranks when he was in drink!...

Did he not one day take it into his head to make her climb to the turret of the belltower with him, right up to the very top, to the summit of the palace!... And what I am telling you is no fairy-story, two hundred thousand inhabitants of Provence saw him. You may imagine the poor mule's terror when, after an hour climbing blindly up a spiral staircase and scaling heaven knows how many steps, she found herself suddenly out on a platform in dazzling sunlight and the whole of Avignon a thousand feet below her looking very strange with market stalls no bigger than hazel nuts, the pope's soldiers like red ants in front of their barracks and over there on a silver thread a microscopic little bridge where they were dancing, dancing... Oh, that poor animal! What a panic! All the windows in the palace shook with her braying.

'What's the matter? What are they doing to her?' cried the pope, rushing on to his balcony.

But Tistet Védène was already in the courtyard, pretending to wail and tear his hair:

'Oh, Holy Father, what a to-do! Your mule ... Oh dear heavens, what will become of us? Your mule has climbed up into the turret ...'

'All by herself???'

'Yes, Holy Father, all by herself, right up to the top ... Can you see the tips of her ears sticking up? They look like two swallows ...'

'Mercy on us!' said the poor pope, raising his eyes ... 'She must have lost her senses! She will be killed! ... Come down, you poor thing!'

The poor beast! Come down was all she wanted to do, but how? There was no question of the staircase; it might be possible to get up a thing like that but you could break your leg a hundred times if you tried to descend ... And the poor giddy mule with her great wild eyes thought about Tistet Védène as she prowled back and forth in desperation on the platform:

'Ah, you rascal, if I ever escape ... what a kick you will get tomorrow morning!'

The thought of kicking him restored her courage a little. Otherwise she would not have withstood the ordeal. Finally they did manage to get her down, but it was a real palaver. They had to use a crane, ropes, and a stretcher. And you can imagine what an indignity it was for a papal mule to be suspended at that height, hooves flailing around in the air, like a maybug on a thread. And the whole of Avignon looking on!

The poor beast did not sleep that night. She felt she was going round and round on that accursed platform with the entire town below laughing at her. Then she thought of that infamous Tistet Védène and of the good kick she was going to deal him the next morning. Oh, my friends, what a kick that would be! You would be able to see the dust rising from as far away as Pampérigouste... Now while she was preparing this fine welcome in her stable, do you know what Tistet Védène was doing? He was sailing down the Rhône on a papal ship, singing all the way to the court in Naples with the band of young nobles that the town sent every year to Queen Jeanne to practise their diplomacy and etiquette. Tistet was not a nobleman. But the pope very much wanted to reward him for the care he had given to his animal and especially for his recent efforts on the day of the rescue.

It was the mule who was disappointed next day!

'Oh what a rogue, he suspects something,' she thought, with a furious shake of her bells... 'but it doesn't matter, you villain; you will get it when you come back, that kick, I'll keep it for you!'

And she did.

After Tistet's departure, the pope's mule again enjoyed the quiet calm of her former rhythms and routines. There was no Quiquet, no Béluguet in the stable any more. The fine days of the wine *à la française* had returned, and with them the good mood, long siestas, and the little gavotting step as she went over the bridge in Avignon. However, since her adventure, the townspeople always treated her a little coolly. People whispered about her as she passed. Old people shook their heads, children laughed and pointed out the belltower to each other. The good pope himself no longer had so much confidence in his friend, and when he relaxed sufficiently to nod off on her back as he returned from the vineyard, the thought was always at the back of his mind: 'Supposing I were to wake up one day up there on the platform!' The mule was pained when she saw that, but she said nothing. Only when the name of Tistet Védène was uttered in her hearing did she twitch her long ears and sharpen her hooves in anticipation on the paving stones.

Seven years went by in this way. Then at the end of those seven years, Tistet Védène came back from the court at Naples. His time there had not yet expired, but he had learned that the pope's Chief Mustard Maker had just died suddenly in Avignon and as the position seemed to him a good one, he had arrived with all speed to be in line for the post.

When the scheming Védène entered the palace room, the Holy Father scarcely recognized him, so much bigger

316 ■ Alphonse Daudet

and more solid had he become. It must be said too that the worthy pope had also aged and that he could not see very clearly without his spectacles.

Tistet was not abashed.

'What, Holy Father, don't you know who I am?... It's me, Tistet Védène!...'

'Védène?'

'Yes, you know... The one who used to take the wine *à la française* to your mule.'

'Oh yes... yes... I remember... A good little chap, that Tistet Védène!... And now, what does he want of us?'

'Oh nothing much, Holy Father... I was coming to ask you... By the way, do you still have your mule? Is she in good health?... Oh, that's good!... I was coming to ask for the position of Chief Mustard Maker, who has just died.'

'You, Chief Mustard Maker! You are too young. How old are you?'

'Twenty years and two months, Your Illustrious Holiness, just five years older than your mule... By God, what a noble animal! If you knew how much I used to love that animal!... How I pined for her in Italy!... Will you not let me see her?'

'Of course you shall see her, my child,' said the good pope, much moved. 'And since you are so fond of this noble animal, it is my wish that you do not live far away from her any longer. From this day on I shall keep you close to me in your capacity as Chief Mustard Maker... My cardinals will object, but that is too bad, I am used to it... Come and find us tomorrow after Vespers and we shall invest you with the emblems of your rank in the presence of our Chapter, and then... I shall take you to see the mule and you shall accompany us both to the vineyard.... Ha! Now be off with you!'

That Tistet Védène was happy when he left the great hall, and with what impatience he was looking forward to the ceremony the next day, I need not tell you. But there was someone in the palace even happier and more impatient than he was. It was the mule. From the time Védène returned until Vespers the next day, the formidable animal gorged constantly on oats, aiming kicks with her back hooves at the wall. She too was preparing for the ceremony...

And so, the next day, when Vespers had been said, Tistet Védène made his entry into the courtyard of the pope's palace. The whole of the high clergy were present, the cardinals in their red robes, the devil's advocate in black velvet, the priests of the monastery with their little mitres, the aediles of Saint-Agrico, the purple gowns of the choir school, the lower clergy too, the pope's soldiers in full uniform, the three brotherhoods of the penitents, the hermits of Mont Ventoux with their wild aspect and the little cleric bringing up the rear carrying his bell, the flagellants naked to the waist, the sacristans resplendent in their judges' robes, all of them, even the dispensers of holy water, and the one who lights the candles and the one who puts them out ... Not one was missing ... Oh, what a fine ordination! Bells, firecrackers, sun, music, and the ever-present *tambourins* leading the dance over there on the bridge at Avignon ...

When Védène appeared in the middle of the Assembly, his fine figure and good looks caused a murmur of admiration. He was a magnificant Provençal specimen, though one of the fair type, with long hair curling at the ends and a dapper little beard which looked as though it had been fashioned from the fine gold shavings of his father's, the goldsmith's, chisel. Rumour had it that the fingers of Queen Jeanne herself had dabbled on occasion in that blonde beard. And my lord Védène did indeed have the triumphant air and distracted look of men who have been loved by queens ... That day, in order to do honour to his nation, Tistet had changed his neapolitan clothes for a jacket edged in a pink Provençal pattern, and on his shoulder, there waved a huge ibis plume from the Camargue.

The moment he entered, the Chief Mustard Maker gave a gallant salute and made his way towards the top of the steps where the pope was waiting to bestow upon him the insignia of his office: the yellow boxwood spoon and the saffron-coloured costume. The mule was at the bottom of the steps, all harnessed up and ready to set off for the vineyard ... When he passed near to her, Tistet Védène smiled kindly and paused to give her two or three little taps on her rump, watching out of the corner of his eye to see if the pope could see him. The situation was perfect. The mule made her move:

'There, take that, you villain! I've been keeping it for you for seven years!'

And she gave him such a terrible terrible kick that even in Pampérigouste they could see the dust of it, a whirl of white dust and in it, floating, the plume of an ibis, all that remained of the unfortunate Tistet Védène! ...

A mule's kicks are not normally so terrifying; but this was the pope's mule. And then, just think! She had been keeping it for seven years ... We shall find no better example of ecclesiastical rancour!

Mateo Falcone

Prosper Mérimée

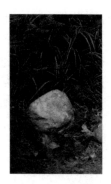

As you leave Porto-Vecchio and head north-west towards the interior of the island you see the land rise quite quickly and after three hours' trek along winding paths obstructed by huge boulders and intersected here and there by ravines, you find yourself on the edge of a very large area of *maquis*. The *maquis* is home to Corsican shepherds and to whoever has got on wrong side of the law. You probably know that the Corsican peasant sets fire to a certain amount of woodland to save himself the trouble of manuring his land; if the flames spread further than they need to, so what? If they do, they do. He is sure of a good harvest if he sows seed on this soil fertilized by the ashes of the trees that once grew there. When the corn is harvested—the stalks, which would be too awkward to remove, are left—the roots of the trees, which remain in the earth without being burned by the fire, send out dense new growth the following spring and in a very few years reach to a height of seven or eight feet. It is this kind of dense undergrowth that is known as the *maquis*. It consists of different species of trees and bushes, variously mixed together as the Almighty pleases. A man can make his way through it only with an axe, and some *maquis* are so dense as to be impenetrable, even by the moufflons.

If you have killed a man, make for the *maquis* of Porto-Vecchio and you will be safe, as long as you have a decent gun and powder and ammunition, and don't forget to take a brown cloak with a hood, which you can use as both blanket and mattress. The shepherds will provide you with milk, cheese, and chestnuts, and you will have nothing to fear from the law or the relatives of the dead man except when you go down to the town to replenish your ammunition.

When I was in Corsica in 18— Mateo Falcone's house was half a league away from this *maquis*. He was quite a rich man for those parts. He lived like a lord off what his flocks produced—that is, he did nothing, while the herdsmen, who were more or less nomadic, took them to graze in various parts of the mountain. When I saw him two years after the event which I am about to relate, he seemed to me at the very most fifty years old. Imagine a small but sturdy man with curly hair, black as jade, an aquiline nose, thin lips, large bright eyes, and a complexion the colour of boot leather. His skill with a gun was legendary even in that part of the world where there are so many good marksmen. Mateo for instance would never have fired at a moufflon with buckshot; but at a hundred and twenty paces he could have laid it low with a single ball either to the head or the shoulder, as he chose. He could use his weapons at night just as well as by day and I was told about a particular skill he had, which may seem scarcely credible to someone who has not travelled in Corsica. A lighted candle would be placed eighty paces away, behind a piece of transparent paper as large as a plate. He would take aim with his gun, the flame would be extinguished, and after a minute in total darkness, Mateo would pull the trigger and pierce that paper three times out of four.

For such exceptional merit Mateo Falcone had won a fine reputation. It was said that he was a good friend but a dangerous enemy. A neighbourly man, he gave to the poor and lived in peace with everyone in the district of Porto-Vecchio. But it was recounted of him that once when he had taken up with a woman in Corte, he had forcefully disposed of a rival who was said to be as formidable in war as he was in love. At least, it was believed to be Mateo who fired a certain shot that took that man by surprise as he shaved at a small mirror which hung from his window. Once the whole affair had died down Mateo married. His wife Giuseppa first bore him three daughters, which infuriated him, and finally a son, whom he named Fortunato: he was the white hope of the family, the inheritor of the family name. The girls were married off satisfactorily: their father could count on the daggers and blunderbusses of his sons-in-law if necessary. The son was only 10 but already showed great promise.

One autumn day Mateo went out early with his wife to go and see to one of his flocks in a clearing in the *maquis*. Young Fortunato wanted to go with them but the clearing was too far off. Besides, someone had to stay behind to look after the house. So the father refused. We shall see if he had cause to rue that decision.

He had been gone for some hours and young Fortunato was quietly lying in the sun gazing up at the blue mountains and thinking how next Sunday he would be going to his uncle, the corporal's, house in town, to have supper, when suddenly his meditations were interrupted by the report of a firearm. He got up and looked in the direction of the plain where this noise had come from. More gunshots followed; they were let off at irregular intervals, and were getting nearer and nearer; at last on the path which led from the plain to Mateo's house there appeared a man in a pointed cap, such as those worn by mountain dwellers; he had a beard and ragged clothing, and was dragging himself painfully along, leaning on his gun. He had just been shot in the thigh.

This man was a bandit who, having left at night to go and fetch gunpowder from the town, had been ambushed by a patrol of Corsican foot-soldiers. After putting up a strong defence he had retreated and fled, hotly pursued but firing from one rock and another as he went. But he did not have much advance on the soldiers and his wound would prevent him from reaching the *maquis* before they caught up with him.

He approached Fortunato and said:

'Are you Mateo Falcone's son?'

'Yes.'

'My name is Gianetto Sanpiero. I am being followed by the yellownecks. Hide me, I cannot go any further.'

'What will my father say if I hide you without his permission?'

'He'll say you did the right thing.'

'How do you know that?'

'Quick, hide me! They're coming.'

'Wait till my father gets back.'

'Wait? Damn you, they will be here in five minutes. Come on, hide me or I'll kill you.'

Fortunato coolly replied:

'Your gun is empty and you don't have any cartridges left in your *carchera*.'

'I have my stiletto.'

'But you can't run as fast as I can.'

And he jumped out of reach.

'You are not Mateo Falcone's son! Would you let me be arrested in front of your house?'

This seemed to strike home.

'What will you give me if I hide you?' asked the boy, coming nearer again.

The bandit fumbled in a leather purse that was hanging from his belt, and took out a five franc coin that he had no doubt been saving to buy gunpowder. Fortunato brightened up at the sight of the coin; he seized it and said to Gianetto:

'Don't be afraid.'

At once he made a large hole in a pile of hay that was next to the house. Gianetto disappeared into it, and the boy covered him in such a way as to leave him breathing space, yet without it being possible to suspect that anyone was hiding in there. In fact he showed some primitive cunning. He took a cat and her kittens and settled them on the pile of hay to make it look as if it had not been touched for a while. Then, noticing there were traces of blood on the path next to the house, he covered them carefully with dust, and, calm and collected, lay down in the sun again.

A few minutes later six men in brown uniform with yellow collars, commanded by an adjutant, were in front of Mateo's door. This adjutant was distantly related to Falcone. (In Corsica, as is well known, family relations are traced much more widely than they are elsewhere.) His name was Tiodoro Gamba. He was an energetic man greatly feared by bandits, several of whom he had hunted down.

'Hello little cousin,' he said, addressing himself to Fortunato. 'My word, how big you've grown! Did you see a man go by just now?'

'Oh, I'm still not as big as you, cousin,' replied the boy, in a foolish tone.

'Give it time. But, tell me now, did you see a man go by?'

'Did I see a man go by?'

'Yes, a man with a pointed black velvet hat and an embroidered red and yellow jacket?'

'A man with a pointed black velvet hat and an embroidered red and yellow jacket?'

'Yes, be quick and tell me, and don't keep repeating my questions.'

'This morning the priest passed by on his horse Piero. He asked me how papa was and I said...'

'Don't try to be clever with me! Tell me which way Gianetto went, because he's the one we are after and I'm sure he went along this path.'

'Who knows?'

'Who knows? *I* know that you have seen him.'

'How can you see anyone passing by when you are asleep?'

'You weren't sleeping, you little villain! You were woken up by the guns.'

'So, cousin, you think your guns make as much noise as all that? My father's pistol is much louder.'

'Go to the devil, you good for nothing! I am certain you have seen Gianetto. Perhaps you've even hidden him. Come on boys, let's get inside the house and see if our man is there. He was only limping along and the rogue has too much sense to try to reach the *maquis* on one leg. Besides, this is where the trail of blood ends.'

'But what will Papa say?' jeered Fortunato. 'What is he going to say when he finds out someone has entered his house while he was out?'

'You good-for-nothing!' said the adjutant Gamba, tweaking his ear. 'Don't you realize I have the power to make you change your tune? Perhaps twenty blows with the back of my sabre will finally make you talk.'

Fortunato continued jeering at him.

'Do you realize, you little wretch, that I can take you to Corte or Bastia. I'll make you lie on straw in a cell with your legs in irons and I'll have your head chopped off if you don't tell me where Gianetto Sanpiero is.'

The boy laughed out loud at this ridiculous threat. He said again:

'My father is Mateo Falcone!'

'Adjutant,' muttered one of the soldiers, 'let's not get on the wrong side of Mateo.'

It was evident that Gamba was in a quandary. He chatted quietly with his soldiers, who had already inspected the whole house. This was not a very long operation, for a Corsican *cabane* consists of only one square room. A table, benches, chests, and firearms or household equipment is the sum total of its furnishings. Meanwhile, young Fortunato stroked the cat and seemed to be taking a malicious pleasure in causing his cousin and the soldiers embarrassment.

A soldier went up to the pile of hay. He saw the cat and gave the hay a desultory poke with his bayonet, shrugging his shoulders, as though he felt this was a stupid thing to try. Nothing moved. And the boy's face betrayed not a flicker of emotion.

The adjutant and his soldiers were giving up and had started to look seriously in the direction of the plain as if inclined to go back the way they had come, when their commander, convinced that threats would make no impression on Falcone, made a last effort to see what he might achieve with cajolery and bribery.

'Little cousin,' he said, 'you seem to me a lad with all his wits about him! You will go far. But you are playing a dangerous game with me, and if I were not afraid of causing pain to my cousin, Mateo, I'd carry you off, damn me if I wouldn't.'

'Pooh!'

'But when my cousin comes back, I'll tell him about this and he'll whip you till you bleed for telling me such lies.'

'You think so?'

'You'll see ... But come on, be a good boy and I'll give you a little something.'

'And I'll give you a piece of advice, cousin. If you stay any longer Gianetto will be in the *maquis* and then it will take more than one of your sort to find him.'

The adjutant took a silver watch worth at least ten crowns out of his pocket, and seeing that young Fortunato's eyes shone when he caught sight of it, he said, dangling the watch on the end of its steel chain:

'You young rascal! Wouldn't you like to have a watch like this one hanging round your neck and strut through the streets of Porto-Vecchio, proud as a peacock, and people saying "What time is it?" and you saying "Take a look at my watch." '

'When I'm grown up my uncle the corporal will give me a watch.'

'Agreed. But your uncle's son has already got one. Not as fine as this one, it's true, but he's younger than you.'

The boy sighed.

'Well, little cousin, do you want this watch or not?'

Fortunato, observing the watch out of the corner of his eye, looked like a cat who has been offered a whole chicken. Sensing that it is being teased, it does not dare to extend a paw and from time to time it averts its gaze so as not to expose itself to temptation. But all the time it licks its lips and seems to be saying to its master 'What a cruel joke you're playing on me!'

The adjutant Gamba nonetheless seemed to be perfectly in earnest about offering him his watch. Fortunato did not put out his hand, but said to him with a sour smile:

'Why are you teasing me?'

'For God's sake, I am not teasing. Just tell me where Gianetto is and this watch is yours.'

Fortunato allowed himself a smile of disbelief; and, fixing his black eyes on those of the adjutant, he attempted to guess from his expression how much trust he might put in his words.

'Strip me of this,' cried the adjutant, touching his epaulette, 'if I do not give you the watch as your reward! My men are witnesses, and I cannot go back on my word.'

So saying, he moved the watch nearer and nearer so that it was almost touching the boy's pale cheek. On the latter's face you could see the inward struggle he was having between greed and the duty to give shelter. His bare chest heaved; he seemed to be almost suffocating. The watch swung back and forth, round and round, and sometimes bumped against the tip of his nose. Then at last, little by little, his right hand rose towards the watch. His finger tips touched it, and he felt the entire weight of it in his hand without the adjutant letting go the end of the chain. The face of it was sky-blue, the case newly furbished, it seemed to blaze in the sun, the temptation was too strong.

Fortunato raised his left hand also and pointed with his thumb, over his shoulder, at the pile of hay he was leaning against. The adjutant understood him straight away. He let the end of the chain drop and Fortunato realized he was the sole possessor of the watch. He sprang up with the agility of a doe and got ten paces away from the pile of hay which the soldiers had immediately begun to demolish.

Very soon the hay was seen to move and a man, still bleeding, emerged with a knife in his hand. But when he tried to stand, his wounded leg, which had stiffened, would not hold him. He fell. The adjutant leaped upon him and seized his stiletto. Immediately he was bound tight, though he struggled.

Gianetto, now prostrate on the ground and tied up like a bundle of faggots, turned his head towards Fortunato, who had come nearer again.

'Son of a . . . ,' he said, more in scorn than anger.

The boy threw back the silver coin he had given him, realizing that he no longer deserved it, but the outlaw did not even seem to notice this gesture. He said to the adjutant with a good deal of sang-froid:

'My dear Gamba, I cannot walk, you will have to carry me into town.'

'You were running faster than a roebuck just now,' his cruel captor replied. 'But don't worry, I'm so pleased to have caught you I could carry you for a league on my back without getting tired. Besides, my friend, we shall make you a litter with branches and your cape and we shall get some horses at Crespoli's farm.'

'Good,' said the prisoner. 'Put a bit of hay on your litter as well to make me more comfortable.'

While the soldiers were busy, some fabricating a kind of stretcher with chestnut branches, others putting a dressing on Gianetto's wound, Mateo Falcone and his wife appeared suddenly at the bend in the road that led to the *maquis*. The woman came nearer, bent painfully under the weight of an enormous bag of chestnuts, while her husband walked along in a carefree way carrying nothing but a gun in his hand and another slung across his chest. It is beneath a man's dignity for him to carry any burden except his weapons.

Mateo's first thought on seeing the soldiers was that they had come to arrest him. But why should they do that? Was Mateo in trouble with the law? No, he enjoyed a good reputation. He was, as they said, a *most reputable individual.* But he was Corsican and he was a man of the mountains and there are few mountain dwellers who, when they search their memories, do not discover some peccadillo like shootings, knifings, or other such trifles. Mateo, more than other men, had a clear conscience, for he had not pointed his gun at anyone for ten years. But all the same he was a prudent man and he prepared to put up a good defence should it prove necessary.

'Wife,' he said to Giuseppa, 'put down your bundle and be ready.'

She obeyed instantly. He gave her the gun from off his shoulder which might have got in his way. He loaded the one he had in his hand and slowly approached his house, going along by the trees which grew by the path, ready at the slightest show of hostility to throw himself behind the thickest trunk, where he could shoot from cover. His wife was at his heels, carrying his spare gun and his cartridge pouch. The duty of a wife in case of combat is to load her husband's weapons.

The adjutant on the other hand was more than anxious when he saw Mateo advancing so deliberately, with his gun levelled and his finger on the trigger.

'What if,' he thought, 'Mateo turned out by chance to be related to Gianetto or was his friend and wanted to protect him, the contents of those two guns of his would reach a couple of us as sure as posting a letter in the box, and what if, notwithstanding the family connection, he were to aim at me...!'

In his uncertainty he came to a very courageous decision: he would go up to Mateo on his own and tell him what had taken place, greeting him like an old acquaintance. But the short distance between him and Mateo seemed inordinately long.

'Hey there, my old comrade,' he cried. 'How goes it, old chap? It's me, Gamba, your cousin.'

Mateo, without uttering a word, had halted and gently, as the other was speaking, he raised the barrel of his gun so that it was pointing to the sky at the moment the adjutant reached him.

'Good day, brother,' said the adjutant holding out his hand. 'I haven't seen you in a very long time.'

'Good day, brother!'

'I passed by to say hello to you and cousin Pepa. We have done a long stint today, but we can't complain about being tired because we have made a famous catch. We have just captured Gianetto Sanpiero.'

'God be praised,' exclaimed Giuseppa. 'He stole a milk goat from us last week.'

These words delighted Gamba.

'Poor devil!' said Mateo. 'He must have been hungry.'

'The villain defended himself like a lion,' continued the adjutant, somewhat mortified. 'He killed one of my men and, not satisfied with that, he broke corporal Chardon's arm. But that wasn't so serious, he was only a Frenchman... Then he hid himself so well, the devil himself wouldn't have found him. But for my little cousin Fortunato I should never have discovered where he was.'

'Fortunato!' exclaimed Mateo.

'Fortunato!' repeated Giuseppa.

'Yes. Gianetto had hidden under that pile of hay over there. But my young cousin showed me the trick he was playing on me. I shall tell his uncle, the corporal, so he can send him a nice present for his trouble. And his name and yours will be in the report I send to the Prosecutor.'

'Go to hell!' said Mateo under his breath.

They had rejoined the rest of the company. Gianetto was already lying on the litter ready to leave. When he saw

Mateo with Gamba and his men, Gianetto gave a strange smile. Then, turning to the door of his house, he spat at the threshold and said:

'House of a traitor!'

Only a man already certain to die would have dared utter the word 'traitor' where Falcone was concerned. A good thrust of a stiletto, which would not have needed repeating, would have been the immediate payment for that insult. But Mateo did no more than put his hand to his forehead like a man stricken.

Fortunato had gone inside when he saw his father coming. He soon reappeared with a bowl of milk that he offered with lowered eyes to Gianetto.

'Get away from me!' shouted the prisoner in a voice like thunder.

Then, turning to one of the soldiers:

'Comrade, give me something to drink,' he said.

The soldier put his gourd into his hands and the bandit drank the water given him by a man with whom he had just exchanged gunfire. Then he asked them to tie his hands in such a way that they were crossed on his breast, instead of behind his back.

'I like,' said he 'to be lying comfortably.'

They made haste to comply. Then the adjutant gave the signal to leave, bade farewell to Mateo, who did not reply, and went rapidly down towards the plain.

338 ■ Prosper Mérimée

It was almost ten minutes before Mateo opened his mouth. The boy anxiously eyed now his mother, now his father, who, leaning on his gun, contemplated him with a look of concentrated anger.

'You've made a fine start!' said Mateo finally in a voice that was calm, but terrifying to those who knew him well.

'Father!' cried the boy, coming forward with tears in his eyes as if to throw himself at his feet.

But Mateo shouted:

'Keep your distance!'

And the boy stopped short, sobbing, motionless, some paces away from his father.

Giuseppa approached. She had just seen the watch chain, one end of which was showing under Fortunato's shirt.

'Who gave you that watch?' she asked severely.

'My cousin, the adjutant.'

Falcone seized the watch and threw it violently against a stone. It smashed into a thousand pieces.

'Wife,' he said, 'is this child mine?'

Giuseppa's brown cheeks turned brick red.

'What are you saying, Mateo? Do you know who you are talking to?'

'Well, this child is the first of his family to betray someone.'

Fortunato's sobs and hiccoughs got worse and Falcone kept his eyes like a lynx fixed on him. Finally he hit the ground with the butt of his rifle, threw it across his shoulder and took the path back to the *maquis*, shouting to Fortunato to follow him. The boy obeyed.

Giuseppa ran after him and caught hold of his arm.

'It's your son,' she said in a shaking voice, fixing her black eyes upon those of her husband as if to read what was going on in his mind.

'Leave me,' said Mateo. 'I am his father.'

Giuseppa kissed her son and went back into her house, crying. She threw herself in front of an image of the Virgin and prayed fervently. Falcone, however, walked some two hundred paces along the path and did not stop till he got to a small ravine and went down into it. He tested the earth with the butt of his rifle and found it soft and easy to dig. The place seemed suitable for his purpose.

'Fortunato, go over to that large stone.'

The boy did as he was told, then fell to his knees.

'Say your prayers.'

'Father, father, don't kill me.'

'Say your prayers!' repeated Mateo in a dreadful voice.

The boy, stuttering, sobbing, recited the *pater* and the *credo*. His father, in a loud voice, responded with an *amen* loudly at the end of each prayer.

'Are those all the prayers you know?'

'I know the *Ave Maria* too and the litany that my aunt taught me.'

'It's long, but no matter.'

The boy got to the end of the litany in a faint voice.

'Have you finished?'

'Oh father, mercy, forgive me. I'll never do it again! I'll beg my cousin the corporal to spare Gianetto!'

He was still speaking. Mateo had charged his gun and aimed it, saying:

'May God forgive you!'

The boy made a desperate effort to get up again and embrace his father's legs, but he did not have time. Mateo pulled the trigger and Fortunato fell down dead.

Without a glance at the body, Mateo went back along the path to his house to get a spade to bury his son. He had gone scarcely a few steps when he met Giuseppa who was running, alarmed by the gunshot.

'What have you done?' she cried.

'Justice.'

'Where is he?'

'In the ravine. I am going to bury him. He died a Christian. I shall have a mass said for him. Tell my son-in-law Tiodoro Bianchi to come and live with us.'

Notes on the Stories

1. **Bretagne** Annie Saumont, born in 1927 in Normandy, is the doyenne of French short-story writing and has won many prizes. This ghost story is set near Dol-de-Bretagne in the frontier area of Brittany, between Rennes, where the narrator's court appearance takes place, and Saint-Malo on the coast, not far from Mont-Saint-Michel. In the Second World War Saint-Malo was badly bombed by the liberating forces and completely rebuilt after 1944 in the original granite, stone by stone. The game of *belote*, played by the travellers on the train, is a card game similar to poker which was particularly in vogue at the time.

2. **Basse-Normandie** Daniel Boulanger was born in Picardy in 1922, and is known for his screenplays as well as for his sketches of provincial life. Bayeux is famous for the tapestry (possibly made in 1077) which depicts William the Conqueror's invasion of Britain in 1066. It is displayed there in the museum. Boulanger is probably referring to the trees in the tapestry that William orders to be cut down to make ships for the invasion. There is a statue of William in the square in Falaise in Normandy.

3. **Haute-Normandie** Guy de Maupassant, 1850–93, was possibly France's greatest short-story writer. This story takes place in the Normandy countryside about 20 kilometres to the west of Rouen, whose cathedral spire is 151 metres high. Himself a

native of this region, and a great traveller, on foot or by coach, Maupassant often wrote satirical stories about Normandy and its inhabitants. The saints Osymus and Pamphilius, who are supposed to cure the pilgrims, are deliberately chosen by the writer for their obscurity.

4. **Nord-Pas-de-Calais** Christian Garcin was born in Marseille in 1959. Lille is northern France's largest city, with all the problems of poverty and racial conflict, and high crime rates that usually go with large connurbations. Nevertheless it has a modern metro system, residential squares, a restored old quarter, plenty of good restaurants and night life, and a strong cultural identity. The artist referred to in the story, Ary Scheffer, was a nineteenth-century Dutch painter who lived for a time in what is now the Musée de la Vie Romantique in Paris. His painting *The Dead Go Quickly* dates from 1830. Barbara Kruger, born in 1945, is an American conceptual artist famous for her 'layered' photographs and collages.

5. **Picardie** The battleground of the First World War, where Pierre Mac Orlan (1882–1970) lived and fought. In this extract from Mac Orlan's writings about the war in Picardy, he views the horror of the trenches through the eyes of a poet. 'Bambara' is the name of an animistic tribe from Mali. The 420 he refers to was almost certainly the famous Big Bertha, the 420mm German howitzer, and the *drachen* (German for 'kite' or 'dragon') was a German observation balloon. The trenches were given names. In the story Aunt Sally and Hollow Way are rough English equivalents.

6. **Île-de-France** Marcel Aymé was born in Burgundy in 1902 and died in 1967. This story about the plight of an Arab in Paris dates from 1943, but seems just as relevant to our own times. Because of France's former colonial connections in Africa, many immigrants live in Paris and Marseille. Arbi lives in the run-down area of the eighteenth *arrondissement* of Paris, north

of the Gare du Nord. The wife of the café owner is probably reading a review of *Beau Geste*, the famous 1939 film about the Foreign Legion, starring Gary Cooper. The song *Mon Légionnaire* was made famous by Edith Piaf.

7. **Champagne Ardenne** The first of two tributes from *Pastorales de Guerre* by Stéphane Émond, born 1964, to his ancestors from the Argonne in Champagne and Lorraine, who fought and suffered in the First World War. *L'Illustration* is the French photographic magazine dating from the mid-nineteenth century that documented many of the battles and events of the war between 1914 and 1918. Gabriele d'Annunzio (1863–1938) was an Italian poet and novelist from the Abruzzi who fought in the First World War for the Allies and went on to become a Fascist under Mussolini.

8. **Lorraine** *House in the Woods*, a strikingly visual text, is again set in the First World War. The story here is told from a mother's point of view.

9. **Alsace** Didier Daeninckx was born in 1949 in the Île-de-France region. His story, set in Strasbourg in the much-disputed region between France and Germany, also has overtones of the war, this time the Second World War. Oradour-sur-Glane in the Haute-Vienne was the site of a particularly horrifying massacre by the SS on 10 June 1944, involving many soldiers from Alsace, when victims were locked in a church which was then burned down. Hans Arp (1887–1966) was a Dadaist poet, painter, and sculptor from Strasbourg. Theo van Doesburg (1883–1931) was a Dutch painter and architect. Jean-Baptiste André Godin, the manufacturer of stoves and a disciple of Fourier, was the founder of a phalanstery, a community settlement. There is a statue of him in Guise in Picardy. The BNP is the Banque Nationale de Paris.

10. **Pays-de-la-Loire** René Bazin was born in Angers in the Loire region in 1853 and died in Paris in 1932. He travelled widely

through France, writing journals and stories. Here, on his home territory, he recounts the story of recent viticulture and how the white grapes were saved for future generations after the disease phylloxera struck. The *vitis rupestris* and the *vitis riparia* are vines grafted from North American stocks. Luigi Calamatta (1802–69) was an Italian engraver and friend of the artist Ingres, and took part in the 1830 revolution mentioned in Bazin's story.

11. **Centre** Another story by Boulanger, *The Cattle Man*, is set near Senonches, known as the 'pearl of the Perche', 40 kilometres from Chartres. It is a small, quiet town in the centre of France, surrounded by lakes, ponds, parks, and woods. One of the visits advertised on the official website is a 'visite des lavoirs' (the communal washing areas still to be seen in many French villages and towns).

12. **Bourgogne** Colette (Sidonie-Gabrielle Colette de Jouvenel, 1873–1954) remained all her life greatly attached to the village of Saint-Sauveur-en-Puisaye in Burgundy where she was born and spent her early childhood, and she returned frequently to her home in her writings. The château in the village has a museum dedicated to the writer. The Poplar Admiral, Purple Emperor, and Scarce Swallowtail are all butterflies.

13. **Franche-Comté** Louis Pergaud, little known to an English-speaking public, was born in 1882 in this region and died in combat in 1915. The Jura mountains, where the story takes place, cover most of the Franche-Comté, which formerly belonged to the dukes of Burgundy and became properly French only in the late seventeenth century. The medieval town of Poligny is particularly known for its cheese-making; the *meule* of cheese on the table of the two characters in the story was once commonly used in payment to tax-collectors. Arbois is the capital of the region's viticulture, producing such specialized wines as *poulsard*, mentioned in the story, *vin de*

paille, dried on straw, and a wine flavoured with walnuts called *vin jaune*.

14. **Poitou-Charentes** Jacques Chardonne (1884–1968) was a Nazi sympathizer, arrested and imprisoned in Jarnac for a short time after the Liberation. He is known as a 'romancier du couple' because he wrote frequently about the marriage relationship. He was born in the south of the Charentes region, in Barbézieux, and many of his works are set in this area. Of the towns mentioned in his story, Cognac is well-known for the production of brandy and *pineau des charentes*; Jarnac, originally a Gallo-Roman settlement, is famous in more recent history as the birthplace of François Mitterand. Royan was destroyed by Allied bombs in 1945 and gradually rebuilt in the 1950s.

15. **Limousin** Claude Michelet was born in Brive-la-Gaillarde in the Limousin in 1938. Brive is a walled city south of Limoges in the *département* of Corrèze. The second part of its name, which means something like 'hearty' or 'lusty', was given it as recently as 1919 and perhaps refers to the strength of its walls, but may also be associated with events during the First World War. Michelet was formerly a farmer in the region; his father Edmond was a resistance fighter and there is a museum in the town bearing his name. Le Vau and Mansart were famous seventeenth-century architects. The *sans-culottes*, distinguishable by their costume, was the name given to the working-class revolutionaries of 1789.

16. **Auvergne** Maupassant visited the Auvergne and stayed in Châtel-Guyon in 1883. This story, with its evocation of the medieval Château de Murol and Lake Pavin, probably derives, like the story *A Norman*, from Maupassant's personal experience. The chapel of pilgrimage that he mentions is eight kilometres to the west of Besse-en-Chandesse, not far from Saint-Nectaire. Lake Pavin, a volcanic lake, is 100 metres deep in places.

17. **Rhône-Alpes** Paul Hervieu, 1857–1915, better known as a novelist and playwright, was born and died in Paris, but the local knowledge he displays in this dramatic story set in the Alps, not far from Mont Blanc, is impressive. The region shares a frontier with both Switzerland and Italy.

18. **Aquitaine** The long straight roads of Aquitaine, edged with pine trees, are characteristic of this region which stretches down as far as the Basque country and the Pyrenees. Anne-Marie Garat, born in 1946, is a novelist and teacher of cinema and has won several prizes for her work, which includes *Aden* (Prix Fémina) and *Les Mal Famées* (Prix Marguerite Audoux).

19. **Midi-Pyrénées** Zola's story is based upon a disastrous flood of the Garonne river near Toulouse, 22 June 1875, when about one thousand people lost their lives. The description of Cyprien's death was inspired by an article in the magazine *L'Illustration* in that year. Saint-Cyprien is an area of Toulouse. Émile Zola, better known for his novels, which include the famous Rougon-Macquart cycle, was born in Paris in 1840 and died there in 1902.

20. **Languedoc-Roussillon** Alphonse Daudet was born in 1840 in Nîmes and died in Paris in 1897. His *Lettres de mon Moulin* (1869), stories purporting to have been written from a windmill in Provence, are perhaps now not so well known as they were when they were first published, or indeed in the mid-twentieth century when the book was commonly read in French classes in British schools. 'Daudet's Windmill' was built in 1814, has been restored, and may be visited. The town of Beaucaire is just inside the regional border of Languedoc.

21. **Provence-Alpes-Côte d'Azur** Daudet's story about the Pope's mule from his collection *Lettres de mon Moulin* is set in Avignon at the time of the Popes, who resided there between 1309 and 1377. It is just inside the border of this region. The wine

Chateauneuf du Pape, which Pope Boniface grows, is still world-famous. A *burette* is a small glass flask used for water or wine in the Mass. A *biretta* is a black cap worn by priests. A *tambourin* is a Provençal drum played with only one drumstick.

22. **Corse** Prosper Mérimée's story of an honour killing, written in 1829, still has the power to shock, not least because in the twenty-first century such customs still exist, if not in Corsica. Mérimée, known chiefly for his stories, was also an inspector of monuments. He was born in 1803 in Paris and died in Cannes in 1870. A *moufflon* is a small wild sheep native to Corsica and Sardinia. A *carchera* is a belt for cartridges.

Selected Further Reading

Collections of short stories

The Oxford Book of French Short Stories, ed. Elizabeth Fallaize (OUP, 2002).

French Short Stories, vols. i and ii, ed. Pamela Lyon and Simon Lee (Penguin, 1966 and 1972).

Short Stories in French, New Penguin Parallel Text, trans. and ed. Richard Coward (Penguin, 1999).

French Stories/Contes français, ed. Wallace Fowlie (Dover Publications, 1990): Ten stories by Voltaire, Balzac, Gide, Camus, and others in a dual language edition.

Great French Short Stories, ed. Paul Negri (Dover Publications, 2004): Twelve stories, including Maupassant and Mérimée.

Selected Short Stories of Balzac, ed. Appelbaum (Dover Publications, 2000).

On the regional background

Pig Earth (Writers and Readers Publishing Cooperative, 1979) and *Once in Europa* (Granta, 1989) by John Berger, in which he shows the changes in French peasant life from village to metropolis.

The Rough Guide to France (9th edn., 2005) has a very useful list of English and French writers who have written about particular areas of France as well as much interesting background material on the regions.

The Discovery of France by Graham Robb (Picador, 2007): a study of the evolution of a nation from the Revolution to the First World War.

The pocket-sized series in French called *Le Goût de...* has fascinating texts and extracts of writing relating to particular towns and regions e.g. *Le Goût de Toulouse*. They are published by Mercure de France and available in most French bookshops.

Publisher's Acknowledgements

1. Bretagne: 'Vous auriez dû changer a Dol', by Annie Saumont, from Festival de la Nouvelle de Saint-Quentin, Direction de la Culture et de l'Animation, Imprimerie Debrez Saint-Quentin, April 2000.

2. Basse-Normandie: Daniel Boulanger, 'Fait pour deux', from *L'Été des femmes*. Éditions de la Table Ronde, 1964, Éditions Gallimard 1985.

3. Haute-Normandie: 'Un Normand', by Guy de Maupassant. *Contes et Nouvelles*, preface by Armand Lanoux. Éditions Gallimard 1974.

4. Nord-Pas-de-Calais: 'Les Muets', by Christian Garcin, from *La Neige Gelée ne permettait que de tout petits pas* 2005.

5. Picardie: Pierre Mac Orlan, 'La Somme', from *Les Poissons morts*, illustrations de Gus. Bofa, Paris, Librairie Payot et Cie 1917.

6. Île-de-France: 'Rue de l'Évangile', from 'Derrière chez Martin' 1938, Marcel Aymé, *Nouvelles Complètes*. Quarto Gallimard 2002.

7. Champagne Ardenne: 'Les Âmes légères', from *Pastorales de Guerre*, Le Temps qu'il fait, Cognac.

8. Lorraine: 'La Maison des Bois', from *Pastorales de Guerre* by Stéphane Émond. Le Temps qu'il fait, Cognac.

9. Alsace: 'Le Fantôme de l'arc-en-ciel', from *Main Courante* by Didier Daeninckx. Librio Éditions Verdier, Lagrasse.

10. Pays-de-la-Loire: 'Les Sauveurs du vin blanc', by René Bazin from *Récits de la plaine et de la montagne*. Calmann-Lévy, Paris.

11. Centre: 'L'Homme des boeufs, by Daniel Boulanger, from *Les Noces du Merle*. Éditions de la Table Ronde 1963, Éditions Gallimard 1985.

12. Bourgogne: Colette, 'Où sont les Enfants?', from *La Maison de Claudine*. J. Ferenczi et fils, 1922.

13. Franche-Comté: 'La Disparition mystérieuse', by Louis Pergaud, from *Nouvelles villageoises*, Mercure de France 1969.

14. Poitou-Charentes: 'Julie', by Jacques Chardonne, from *Femmes: contes choisis et quelques images*. A. Michel 1986.

15. Limousin: 'L'Âme des pierres', by Claude Michelet, from *Un toit, nouvelles sur le logement*. Le Cherche-midi for the Fondation Abbé Pierre, May 2006.

16. Auvergne: 'Un humble drame', by Guy de Maupassant, *Contes et Nouvelles*, preface by Armard Lanoux. Éditions Gallimard 1974.

17. Rhône-Alpes: 'Le Taureau du Jouvet', by Paul Hervieu, from *L'Alpe Homicide*. Alphonse Lemerre, Paris 1886.

18. Aquitaine: *On ne peut pas continuer comme ça*, by Anne-Marie Garat. Les éditions de l'Atelier, May 2006.

19. Midi-Pyrénées: 'L'Inondation', by Émile Zola, from *Contes et Nouvelles*. Gallimard, Pléiade.

20. Languedoc-Roussillon: 'La Diligence de Beaucaire', by Alphonse Daudet, from *Lettres de mon Moulin*. Librio.

21. Provence-Alpes-Côte d'Azur: 'La Mule du Pape', by Alphonse Daudet, from *Lettres de mon Moulin*. Librio, Nov. 2003.

22. Corse: *Mateo Falcone*, by Prosper Mérimée. Librio Flammarion.

Although every effort has been made to trace and contact copyright holders prior to publication this has not been possible in every case. If notified, the publisher will be pleased to rectify any omissions at the earliest opportunity.

Regions of France

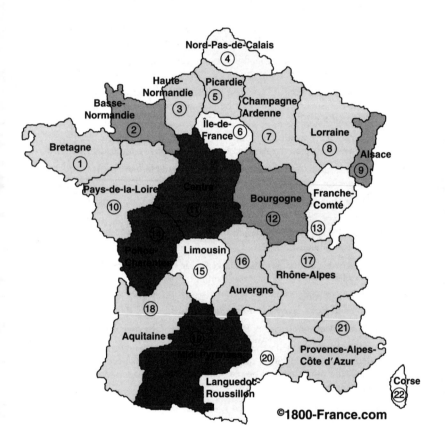

Nord-Pas-de-Calais
④

Haute-Normandie
③

Picardie
⑤

Champagne Ardenne
⑦

Lorraine
⑧

Alsace
⑨

Basse-Normandie
②

Bretagne
①

Île-de-France ⑥

Bourgogne
⑫

Franche-Comté
⑬

Pays-de-la-Loire
⑩

Centre
⑪

Limousin
⑮

Auvergne
⑯

Rhône-Alpes
⑰

Poitou-Charentes
⑲

Aquitaine
⑱

Midi-Pyrénées
⑲

Languedoc-Roussillon

Provence-Alpes-Côte d'Azur
㉑

Corse
㉒

©1800-France.com